HINDUISM

Religious Traditions of the World

Titles available from Waveland Press

Buddhism *by Robert C. Lester*
Confucius *by Herbert Fingarette*
Hinduism *by David M. Knipe*
Islam and the Muslim Community *by Frederick M. Denny*
Myth and Reality *by Mircea Eliade*
Native Religions of North America *by Åke Hultkrantz*
Religion and Culture *by Annemarie de Waal Malefijt*
Religion in Chinese Society *by C. K. Yang*
Religion in Human Life *by Edward Norbeck*
Religions of Africa *by E. Thomas Lawson*
Religions of China *by Daniel L. Overmyer*
Religions of Japan *by H. Byron Earhart*
Religions of Mesoamerica *by David Carrasco*

HINDUISM

Experiments in the Sacred

DAVID M. KNIPE

Prospect Heights, Illinois

For information about this book, write or call:
Waveland Press, Inc.
P.O. Box 400
Prospect Heights, Illinois 60070
(847) 634-0081

Photos courtesy of David M. Knipe
Maps by John Foster

Published by arrangement with HarperSanFrancisco, a division of HarperCollins Publishers, Inc.
1998 reissued by Waveland Press, Inc.

ISBN 1-57766-011-0

Printed in the United States of America

7 6 5 4 3 2

for Susan

Contents

Acknowledgments

Gratitude goes out to many students and colleagues over the years at the University of Wisconsin, to numerous friends and colleagues in different regions of India—Satyanarayana Pandey in Varanasi and M. V. Krishnayya in Waltair in particular—and to mentors and colleagues in Europe and the United States. They have helped to shape my understanding of India and its religions.

To Byron Earhart, editor of this series, and Thomas Grady, my editor, I owe special thanks for their encouragement and patience, and for their care in production I thank also Kevin Bentley, Terri Goff, Joanne Sandstrom, and others on staff.

A portion of this book developed while in India during a fellowship from the American Institute of Indian Studies, and another portion while assisted by the Social Science Research Council, and to both I am indebted.

To my daughers Nicola, Viveka, and Jennifer, and to my wife Susan, warm thanks for sharing the enchantments, conundrums, and gentle hazards of life in Kashi and/or Rajahmundry.

D.M.K.

Chronology of Hinduism in South Asia

PREHISTORY AND THE INDUS VALLEY CIVILIZATION

c. 6500 BCE	Beginnings of agriculture west of the Indus River
c. 3000 BCE	Emergence of pastoral nomad societies in the Deccan
c. 2500 BCE	Emergence of urban societies along the Indus River
c. 2200–2000 BCE	Harappa at its height
c. 2000–1500 BCE	Decline of the Indus civilization; migrations of Indo-Iranian pastoral nomads from Central Asia onto the Iranian plateau and into northwest India

The Vedic Period

c. 1500–1000 BCE	Continuing Indo-Aryan migrations into northwest India
c. 1200 BCE	Composition of the hymns of the *Rigveda*

c. 1200–900 BCE	*Yajurveda, Samaveda, Atharvaveda*
c. 1000–800 BCE	Brahmanas, early Shrauta Sutras; Indo-Aryan migrations eastward across North India; emergence of urban societies along the Ganges River
c. 900–600 BCE	Aranyakas, early Upanishads
c. 600–200 BCE	Later Upanishads, other Sutras dependent on the Vedas
c. 500 BCE	Indo-Aryan migrations southward into Sri Lanka

The Epic Period and Classical Indian Civilization

c. 483 BCE	Traditional date for the death of Siddhartha Gautama, the Buddha
c. 468 BCE	Traditional date for the death of Vardhamana Mahavira, twenty-fourth and last great sage of Jainism
400 BCE–400 CE	Composition of the epic *Mahabharata*
c. 327–325 BCE	Invasion of northwest India by Alexander the Great
c. 324–185 BCE	Maurya dynasty begun by Chandragupta; Ashoka, patron of Buddhism, ruled 272–242
200 BCE–200 CE	Composition of the epic *Ramayana;* consolidation respective of Buddhist and Jaina schools

c. 150–300 CE	Early Dharma Shastras: Manu (Manava), Yajnavalkya
c. 300–500	Early Puranas: Markendeya, Matsya, Vayu, Narasimha, Vishnu, Devi
c. 320–550	Gupta dynasty, India's golden age
c. 450	Tamil epic *Cilappatikaram*
c. 500–700	Early Tantras
c. 500–900	Nayanmar Shaiva poets of Tamil South India
c. 550–750	First Chalukya dynasty of South India
c. 600–930	Alvar Vaishnava poets of Tamil South India
c. 650	Tamil Shaiva Siddhanta schools
c. 800	Manikkavachakar, Tamil Shaiva poet-saint, author of *Tiruvachakam*

THE MEDIEVAL PERIOD

c. 711–715 CE	Arab Muslims invade northwest India
c. 788–820	Traditional dates for Shankara
c. 750–1000	Later Puranas: Vamana, Kurma, Linga, Varaha, Padma, Agni, Garuda, Skanda, Shiva, Bhagavata, Bhavishya, Brahma, Brahmavaivarta, Devibhagavata

c. 850–1279	Chola dynasty of South India
c. 900–1200	Great temples of Khajuraho, Bhubaneswar, Tanjore, Konarak, etc.
c. 1021	Ghaznavid (Turkish) Muslim capital at Lahore; beginning of the decline of Buddhism in India, disappearance by 1550
c. 1056–1137	Traditional dates for Ramanuja
c. 1150	Kampan's *Iramavataram,* a Tamil *Ramayana*
1192	Ghorid Muslim capital at Delhi
c. 1200	Jayadeva's *Gitagovinda;* Virashaivas in South India; early orders of Sufis in North India
1210–1526	Delhi Sultanate
c. 1238–1317	Madhva, founder of the Dvaita school of Vedanta
c. 1300–1350	Muslim conquest of peninsular India; Deccan Sultanates established
1399	Destruction of Delhi by Timur, ruler of Central Asia
c. 1336–1565	The Vijayanagara empire of South India
c. 1400	Villiputtur Alvar's Tamil version of *Mahabharata*

c. 1398–1448	Kabir, North Indian devotional poet
c. 1469–1539	Guru Nanak, founder of Sikhism
c. 1479–1531	Vallabha, founder of sect devoted to Krishna
c. 1483–1563	Surdas, North Indian Hindi devotional poet
c. 1485–1533	Chaitanya, Bengali mystic
1498	Vasco da Gama lands on west coast of India
c. 1498–1546	Mirabai, Rajasthani devotional poetess
1526–1707	Mughal empire, Muslim emperors Babur to Aurangzeb
c. 1532–1623	Tulsidas, author of *Ramcaritmanas* (Hindi *Ramayana*)
1542–1605	Akbar, greatest of Mughal emperors
1608	British East India Company in Surat
c. 1608–1649	Tukaram, poet-saint of Maharashtra
1666–1708	Gobind Singh, tenth and last Sikh Guru
c. 1700	*Kalki,* last of the major Puranas

1739	Destruction of Delhi by Nadir Shah, king of Iran
1757	Battle of Plassey, defeat of Muslim rulers in Bengal by the British East India Company

THE MODERN PERIOD

1772–1833 CE	Ram Mohan Roy; Brahmo Samaj founded 1828.
1858	British viceroy officially replaces Mughal rule in India
1824–1883	Dayananda Sarasvati; Arya Samaj founded 1875
1836–1886	Ramakrishna, Bengali mystic
1863–1902	Vivekananda; Ramakrishna Movement founded 1897
1869–1948	Mohandas Karamchand Gandhi
1861–1941	Rabindranath Tagore, 1913 Nobel laureate for *Gitanjali*
1872–1950	Aurobindo Ghose, philosopher, teacher, founder of religious center in Pondicherry
1877–1938	Muhammad Iqbal; separate Muslim state proposed 1930
1876–1948	Muhammad Ali Jinnah, president of Muslim League; separate states for Muslim majority areas proposed 1940

1879–1951	Ramana Maharshi, mystic of South India
1893	Vivekananda at the World Parliament of Religions in Chicago; Vedanta societies spread in the West
1896–1977	A. C. Bhaktivedanta Swami, founder of International Society for Krishna Consciousness, based in Los Angeles
1926–	Satya Sai Baba
1947	British grant independence to India; migrations of 17 million Hindus, Muslims, and Sikhs; more than a quarter of a million killed during partition of India and the Islamic Republic of Pakistan.
1948	Sri Lanka (Ceylon) granted independence from British rule
1950	Republic of India; Jawarhalal Nehru, first prime minister, 1947–1964
1960s	Maharishi Mahesh Yogi, Bhaktivedanta, and other Indian *gurus* establish eclectic movements in the West
1970s	Hindus in Europe, United States, Canada begin building temples
1971	East Pakistan becomes separate state of Bangladesh
1975	Birendra crowned as tenth Shah ruler of Nepal, the last Hindu kingdom of South Asia

■

CHAPTER I

Introduction

Undergraduate students who are fortunate enough to travel and study in South Asia are almost invariably transformed by their experiences. Typical of most of them, if perhaps more articulate, one such student wrote this testimony following a junior-year study tour.

> In my travels in South Asia I was exposed to things emphatically different from what I had known in the West. Some of the differences were obvious—skin color, language, climate—and some subtle—metaphysical beliefs, perceptions, worldviews. In Asia I saw the most abject poverty imaginable, and became friends with begging lepers; I saw beautiful tropical forests, and shared my lunch with Sherpa children in the Himalayas; I drank tea with Buddhist monks, and discussed the caste system with wandering ascetics. My experiences in Asia unsettled me, and changed the way I see myself, my culture, my society. And of course, these experiences immeasurably altered my view of South Asia.
>
> Oddly, in many ways I feel I know even less about South Asia than I did before I left, for with each new experience emerged layer upon layer of meaning, layer upon layer of understanding. I don't find this at all daunting, for although I know that there are an infinite number of things about South Asian culture I do not know, I also know that there are an infinite number of things I can know. The journal entry for the day I left South Asia consists of a single sentence: "My head is a jumble of possibilities."

We might well employ this enthusiastic undergrad's final phrase as a subtitle for an introductory chapter, for Hinduism does seem to present itself as "a jumble of possibilities," including also the probability that no definition of "Hinduism" will prove satisfactory to all insiders and outsiders. So elusive is this ancient and cumulative religious tradition that some scholars have despaired of definition and suggested that Hindus are identified simply as the religious remainder after one subtracts all Muslims, Jainas, Buddhists, Christians, Jews, Parsis, and tribals from the religious landscape of South Asia. That observation is challenged in this introduction and in the following chapters with a portrayal of the character, extent, and significance of experiences and expressions that have been the dominant feature of South Asian religion for most of the past thirty centuries.

Let us begin with the territory, South Asia. According to those who study plate tectonics and the geological history of our planet, South Asia includes the triangular area that detached itself from southern Africa and sailed off until it crunched into the belly of Asia, forming the Himalayan massif with the impact and becoming what is known as the Indian subcontinent. Historically speaking, South Asia is the equivalent of India, that is, the land the ancient Greeks and Persians declared to be east of the river known in Sanskrit as the Sindhu. Politically speaking, modern South Asia is the large nation of India, that occupies most of that subcontinent, and the several smaller nations immediately adjacent, including Pakistan, Tibet, Nepal, Sikkim, Bhutan, Bangladesh, and the island country off the southeast tip of India, Sri Lanka. One additional modern nation not adjacent but historically and culturally linked to India is Afghanistan. With reference to South Asia today this region is distinguished from West Asia (the Mediterranean coast to Iran), Central or Inner Asia, East Asia (China, Taiwan, Korea, Japan), and Southeast Asia (Burma, Thailand, Cambodia, Laos, Vietnam, Malaysia, and Indonesia). From prehistory to the present the region of South Asia has had significant historical and cultural exchanges with all of these other areas—West, Central, East, and Southeast Asia.

Where religions are concerned, South Asia harbors three dominant faiths, Hinduism, Islam, and Buddhism, and a number of minority religions, including Christianity, Jainism, Parsism (Zoroastrianism), and Judaism. Hindus are to be found in all the nations of South Asia, comprising the dominant tradition of India and Nepal (more than 80% in each), roughly one-fifth of the population of Sri Lanka, and only tiny minorities in Pakistan and Bangladesh, where Islam is the state religion. There are also thriv-

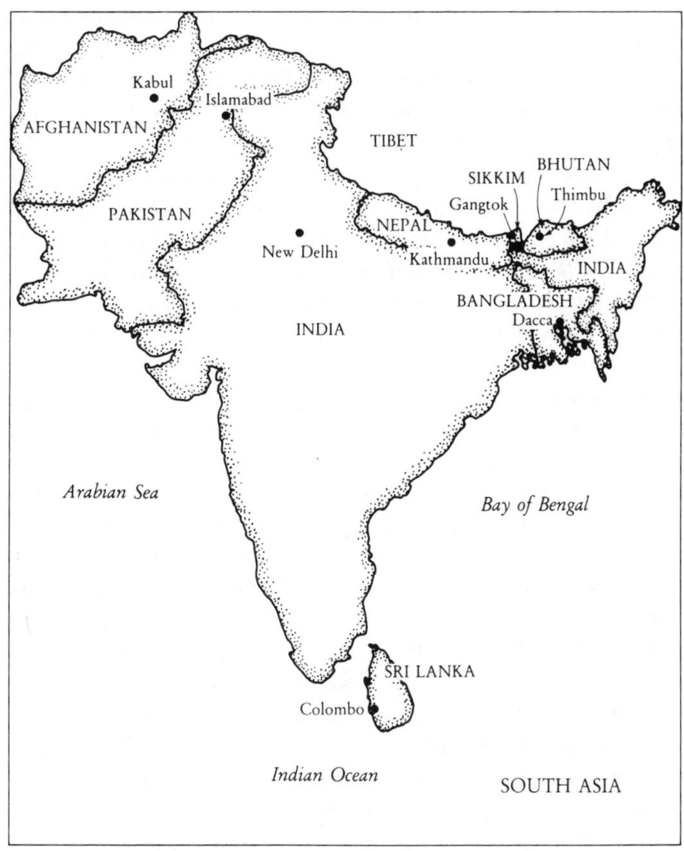

ing Hindu communities outside of South Asia. In Southeast Asia there were large populations of Hindus in the medieval period, but after the advent of Islam only certain enclaves of traditional Hinduism remained, the Indonesian island of Bali being one prominent example. The modern era has witnessed the growth of Hindu populations in many cosmopolitan urban centers in Southeast Asia, including Singapore and Kuala Lumpur on the Malay peninsula, as well as Hong Kong on the south coast of China. Substantial communities of Hindus live in eastern and southern Africa, in the thriving Persian Gulf states, on the island of Fiji in the South Pacific, on the northeast coast of South America, on islands such as Trinidad in the Caribbean and, as the active temples in Pittsburgh, Chicago, Houston, San Francisco, London, and elsewhere may suggest, in many major cities of North America and Europe.

However far-flung these medieval and modern migrations might have been, it remains true that Hinduism is not a multicultural religion to the same extent as Buddhism, Christianity, or Islam. India, the source, remains India, the heartland. In fact, so deep is this identity of a people and a faith that the modern nation of India often finds its credibility tested when declaring itself a religiously plural secular state.

Important for an understanding of a people is a recognition of the land they inhabit and in many respects revere. The great variety of natural regions of the subcontinent explain in part the tremendous cultural and linguistic diversity within the South Asian area. A brief survey of the terrain from north to south is in order.

Separating the subcontinent from Central or Inner Asia is the world's greatest system of mountain peaks and glaciers, the Himalayas, extending west-east for 1,500 miles. In the inhabited plateaus, valleys, and foothills of these mountains are many regions, including the whole of Nepal, where Hinduism, Buddhism, and indigenous folk religions have interacted for many centuries. South of the Himalayas, between the Indus river system in the west and the jungles of Assam in the east, stretch the North Indian or Gangetic plains. This is a zone of intensive cultivation along the rivers Ganges and Jamuna with dense populations in numerous cities and thousands of villages. It is in this region that Hinduism received much of its basic character. In fact modern cities such as Varanasi (also known as Kashi or Banaras), Allahabad (ancient Prayaga), Gaya, and Hardwar remain sacred centers for Hindu pilgrims today, just as they were in ancient times nearly three thousand years ago.

Farther to the south the relatively low-lying Aravalli, Vindhya, and other mountain ranges provide another border declaring a third distinctive region, peninsular India or the Deccan plateau. This vast triangular area is largely savannah bordered by two additional mountain systems, the Western Ghats running along the west coast on the Arabian Sea and the Eastern Ghats fronting the east coast on the Bay of Bengal. The deep south of this peninsular region generated a classical culture and literature quite independent of the north. Already in the early centuries of the Common Era many southern sacred centers became pilgrimage goals on a spiritual chart known throughout the subcontinent. Such a pan-Indian map included the cities known today as Thanjavur, Kanchipuram, Madurai, and other sites such as the ancient temple at Sri Shaila.

In addition to the Indus, Ganges, Jamuna, and Brahmaputra rivers in the north, several great southern rivers cross this Deccan plateau. The Narmada flows west into the Arabian Sea; the Mahanadi, Godavari, and Krishna all run eastward to the Bay of Bengal. Historically, agricultural settlements developed along all of these rivers, and such migration routes linked together the diverse subcultures of South Asia. Furthermore, the rivers themselves became sacred entities and therefore sites of distinguished temples, calendrical festivals, personal rituals, and human transformations.

The physical borders provided by mountains, rivers, forests, and deserts of course had much to do with the historic emergence of intangible borders declared by languages. The subcontinent displays four distinct linguistic families, including the Indo-European, Dravidian, Tibeto-Burman, and Austro-Asiatic. During the second millennium BCE, speakers of Indo-Aryan migrated into northwest India, thereby extending an eastern branch of the Indo-European language family into South Asia. In North India today Hindi, a descendant from ancient Indo-Aryan, is spoken in a variety of dialects as a mother tongue or second language by more than 300 million people, as well as by others in South India. Additional languages of the north include, among others, Marathi, Gujarati, Sindi, Punjabi, Rajasthani, Bengali, and Nepali.

In peninsular India to the south the Dravidian family has been dominant from prehistory; it includes four major languages—Malayalam, Kannada, Telugu, and Tamil. Each of these four dominates a linguistic state of contemporary India (Kerala, Karnataka, Andhra, and Tamil Nadu, respectively), just as the northern states of India from Gujarat to Bengal, plus the separate nation of Nepal, are essentially language zones. Most of the Hindu minority on the island nation of Sri Lanka speaks Tamil rather than Sinhala, the official language and that of the Buddhist majority.

The other two language families of South Asia are much smaller considering the numbers of speakers. The Tibeto-Burman family is represented by languages spoken in the Himalayan and northeastern areas—Newari in the Kathmandu valley, for example, or Lepcha in Sikkim and elsewhere, or Manipuri in the northeast. Austro-Asiatic languages are still spoken by the many tribal peoples of central, eastern, and northeastern India, including the Mundari, Santali, Kherwari, and others.

English, established by the British in the eighteenth and nineteenth centuries as the language of commerce, government, and higher education, is today the language of only about 2 percent of the population of India. That figure sometimes surprises Americans and Europeans who regularly encounter many South Asians who have been fluent in English since childhood.

It may be noted here that the vocabulary of Hinduism is primarily Sanskrit, a "perfected" or "refined" speech, that is to say, a classical form of ancient Indo-Aryan that became, via the learned Brahman elite, the language of the oral traditions of Hinduism. Eventually the ancient oral texts became written texts and inscriptions (as well as continuing oral literatures) after the introduction of various scripts from west Asia late in the first millennium BCE. However, it was not until the early medieval period—about the seventh or eighth century CE—that one of the later scripts, *devanagari,* was widely employed in North India. Never a mother tongue, always a second or third language of the learned, Sanskrit is still spoken today by many priests and scholars. From the Vedic of the *Rigveda* to present-day recitations of medieval Puranas by priests in temples and homes, Sanskrit has remained the fundamental sound of Hinduism. The Glossary at the back of this book provides a brief note on Sanskrit pronunciation and transliteration.

The peoples and cultures of India—ancient or modern—have always been celebrated for a diversity quite as rich as that of their terrain and its varied climates: multiple economies, diets, habitats, clothing, life-styles; today, sixteen official languages, each with multiple dialects, and hundreds of minor tongues; a mind-boggling array of castes, subcastes, tribes, clans, and kinship designations; half a dozen major religions, each with a battery of sects, and tens of thousands of localized cults; nonliterary traditions that, for lack of knowledge and imagination, outside observers sometimes dismiss as "animism." And yet, through all of this vigorous display of geographic, historic, cultural, and linguistic diversity there remains a religious entity, Hinduism, that can in fact be identified and explored.

Hinduism can be seen to develop over a period of more than three thousand years, with significant contributions entering the tradition continuously. Such a breadth of historical experience in addition to multicultural and regional diversity might excuse the Hindu tradition from any concise or simple definition. Nevertheless, a pattern of beliefs and practices emerged over time on which both ancient and modern Hindus might agree.

One concise statement appeared about the beginning of the Common Era in what came to be an authoritative text of classical Hindu law, the Laws of Manu, or Manava Dharma Shastra. Traditionally this Sanskrit text was compiled by the sage **Manu** as one

Indra, king of the gods, on his white elephant Airavata. (Thirteenth-century temple relief, Somnathpuram, Karnataka)

of several digests concerned with religion, law, right conduct—all that is encompassed in the Sanskrit word **dharma**.* Manu declared that a person may concentrate on liberation from the world of continuous rebirths only after paying off three debts. Manu's statement is a good working definition of Hinduism because it focuses upon the central concerns of the ongoing tradition.

The flow of existences is known in classical Hinduism as transmigration **(samsara)**, a dilemma to be solved by release **(moksha)** from bondage to this world brought about by the consequences of action **(karma)**. Manava Dharma Shastra 6.35 reflects the historical development of Hinduism, as well as its powerful conservatism. Manu's phrase combines the individual's three debts, a belief that was already a thousand years old in Manu's day, with the notion that an individual experiences continuous cycles of births and deaths in this world, a more recent doctrine.

Turning first to the older belief, the three debts—to the ancient sages, the gods, and the ancestors—are first described about 1000 BCE in sacred texts known as the Vedas. Three obligations are said to be incurred at birth by everyone in the elite class of priests and scholars known as Brahmans, and they should be paid to the mythical sages who first transmitted the Vedas, to the gods, and to the ancestors or collective "Fathers" as they are known. A Brahman becomes free of this natal liability by learning and reciting the eternal **Vedas** (thereby passing them on as the ancient sages did in the beginning), by sacrificing to the gods (thereby continuing the world that was created by sacrifice in the beginning), and by producing a son (thereby perpetuating a lineage as the Fathers did in the beginning). Freedom from such debts was a spiritual fulfillment, an emancipation from the routine of a householder reciting the three sacred texts and tending his three sacred fires.

By the time the Laws of Manu were compiled, however, several significant transitions had occurred to provide a new context for this belief in three basic obligations. For one, the notion of three debts at birth applied to all three "twiceborn" classes—the Brah-

---

*Terms defined in the Glossary as well as concepts and names that appear on the list of Deities, Powers, and Deified Heroes are printed in boldface where they first appear in text.

mans, the warriors, and the producers. In other words, the whole of the three-level society was involved as a unit distinguished from an alien world outside the authority of these sacred texts and rituals. Second, the worldview in Manu's time was radically altered from the one that had prevailed in 1000 BCE. Attention now focused upon release from bondage to this painful world of *samsara*, upon an adequate means of dealing with the consequences of action, *karma,* a cosmic impersonal accounting that causes rebirth. And third, the Laws of Manu suggest in this same passage that a Brahman householder may transcend domestic life by incorporating his three sacred fires within himself in order to take up the renunciant ascetic path in the forest.

Thus all the ingredients by which classical Hinduism is defined are present in this Laws of Manu segment. *Samsara* and *karma* are basic facts of the human condition, and *moksha* the ultimate aim of the spiritual life. The path toward liberation from the round of births and deaths involves recognition of the eternal Vedas and the ancient sages (**rishis**) who made them available, worship of the gods (**devas**) who created this universe, and responsible regard for the Fathers (**pitrs**) with continuation of their lineage into the future. But the path also involves an idealized fourfold program for life that proceeds from study of the sacred texts—the student (**brahmacarin**) absorbs sacred knowledge (**veda**)— to the life of the married householder (with children, civic responsibilities, and sacred tasks such as worship of the family deities), to the chaste simplicity of the forest-dwelling stage and intensification of the spiritual quest. The fourth and final stage is that of the **samnyasin,** the renunciant who interiorizes his sacred fires and is detached from actions that bind.

Matching this fourfold program of life stages, known as **ashramas,** is a set of four goals of life for every Hindu, also sequential: the pursuits of sexual love (*kama*), wealth or material gain (*artha*), spiritual conduct or duty (*dharma*), and liberation (*moksha*). *Moksha* transcends the preceding three pursuits as the *samnyasin* transcends his previous three life stages.

In the two millennia that separate such classical texts as Manu's from the Hinduism of regional South Asia today a great deal has transpired. Attention shifted from the great body of texts known as Vedas to equally huge collections of epic recitations and performances, as well as other new genres of oral mythology and tradition. The focus on sacrifice in the Vedic mode gradually gave way to worship of and devotional expression to a powerful set of deities including the older gods Vishnu and Shiva and newer goddesses such as Durga or Kali. The structure of society became increasingly complicated as the class hierarchy gave way to a regionally varied and more intensely stratified caste system. And along the way Hinduism was frequently threatened and then benefited by encounters with other faith traditions, including Jainism and Buddhism, and subsequently Christianity, Zoroastrianism, and Islam.

In sum, if we were to identify a Hindu in India, Nepal, or elsewhere in South Asia today, he or she would no doubt believe in *karma* and *samsara,* revere certain sacred texts and certain deities (usually without naming a single text or deity as requisite), accept the obligation of satisfying his or her older ancestors with progeny and with more or less regular offerings and prayers, declare class and caste status within a social structure that most Hindus would recognize, demonstrate certain ascetic tendencies in the form of fasts and vows, and describe certain progress or intentions in life goals and pursuits toward an ultimate release (although for many the ideal of *moksha* is a remote target at the far end of an inevitable series of rebirths).

In other words the broad definition of Hinduism today is very nearly what it was more than two millennia ago in the classical period. Two important changes might be registered here, however. One is the deepening base of Hinduism in the folk and tribal traditions of every region of the subcontinent. Those who were "alien" in the period of the early Vedas and "excluded" in the time of Manu have in many respects come to be the dominant forces in the currents of Hinduism over the millennia, and their traditions are now mingled irreversibly into the mainstream. The other change is to the gender base. We noted that the debt to the Fathers is paid by producing a son (not just a child) according to this male-dominated tradition, and everywhere in Vedic, classical, medieval, and modern Hinduism the paradigms in myths, rituals, doctrines, and symbols are masculine. But just as goddess traditions encroached successfully on the territory of masculine deities, so too has the impact of women's religious activity, the ritual life in particular, been of increasing significance in the overall scale of

Hindu tradition. To put this another way, in traditional life the unlettered folk have always shaped Hinduism, and half of them have been women. It is not feminine roles in Hinduism that have been lacking but rather the acknowledgment of such in literature, the arts, and institutions such as the priesthood and temple and monastic administrations. Only now, in a world rapidly changing because of educational opportunities, are such institutions and media beginning to reflect accurately the total picture of Hindu class, caste, gender, and regional life.

In the following exploration of Hinduism past and present the extraordinary diversity of regions and locales, cultures and subcultures, languages and dialects, sects and cults must be kept foremost in mind. Illustrations cannot be drawn equitably or convincingly from every region or tradition or period, from Nepali-speaking Shaivas in the Himalayas to Tamil-speaking Vaishnavas in Sri Lanka, from Nambudiri Brahmans in Kerala to tribal ritualists in Orissan temples. Therefore a few selected voices must be asked to attempt the impossible, that is, to speak for the many.

■

CHAPTER II

Hinduism and History: Prehistoric and Vedic Periods

Time ripens all beings by itself, in itself. But no one here on earth knows one whom Time has fully ripened.
Mahabharata 12.231.25

Hinduism as a living tradition today has a long and exacting but quite selective memory. It is a tradition that remembers the cumulative experience of ages rather than specific events of a decade or century. Only the Greeks recalled that Alexander and his armies once invaded South Asia, and it was Chinese travelers who retained important details about early Buddhism in India. It is a tradition that prefers to live on cosmic time, not human social calendars. To this day there is often uncertainty about the beginning times of major festivals: the proper moment is eventually divined from the movements of celestial bodies and communicated from the specialists to the public. It is a tradition that seldom remembered the names of its ancient poets and rarely recorded political details, but generated the longest known epic poem about a war that may never have happened. Today many people who routinely recite 108 names of a goddess or a god cannot recall the name of any Hindu ruler before Jawarharlal Nehru became prime minister of India in 1947.

Immediately there is a problem of communication. The contemporary West is a historically minded civilization with a legacy of tough-minded critical inquiry and analysis. "Myth" is depreciated into that which is not true; lines are drawn between past, present, and future; the stuff of human experience is ordered and conclusively paginated, bound, and covered, with HISTORY embossed on the spine. Who wrote this, when did that happen, what happened next? Is this true, or just a myth or legend? When responses to queries such as these tend to collapse time and space, or apply some other frame to the picture, or worse, regard these organizing habits as interesting but irrelevant, it is not unusual for the outsider to lose all bearings.

The following conversation, an illustration, took place in North India when a villager pointed outside his village to an ashen stretch of land where nothing would grow: "A great fire swept through here," he explained. "When did this happen?" asked his American student guest. "Oh, long ago." "How long ago? In the past century?" persisted the American. "Oh, no, much further back, in the time when **Rama** was king." "But isn't Rama a god?" asked the student, who had read a book on Hinduism. "Yes, yes, but here he was also our great king."

How should one consider the countless "long agos" of Hinduism, the timeless tides of mythology, ritual, symbolism that wash over the outlines outsiders try to impose upon them? Communicating with India is a demanding process, and one that favors procedure. A first step is to declare what the tradition says about itself. Second comes an organization of what the tradition says into components that make sense to us as observers, students, investigators, even if inadequacies are recognized in such organization. And third, the meaning of these components is highlighted within the tradition as a whole.

For example, the Vedas are the foremost texts of ancient Hinduism. Vedic tradition says they are a unity existent from eternity and without human origin. That religious fact must be declared first and stated clearly. But outside scholarly curiosity has applied itself to these texts as it has to Aristotle, Shakespeare, and the Bible, and on linguistic and literary grounds determined them to have been composed variously between something close to 1200 and 200 BCE. That organizational and text-critical view must also be provided before moving on to questions of meaning. What is the immediate religious significance of this unity and eternity attributed to the Vedas? What does the Hindu tradition over the long haul do with such notions? Can outsiders learn something by valuing the traditional perspective as much as the analytic one, in other words by allowing space for reflection and dialogue?

The title of this chapter, a prefiguration of dialogue, is not "The History of Hinduism," but "Hinduism and History." A division of Indian experience into historical periods does not come with the territory. There are no sequential dynasties, as in Egypt, Assyria, or China, for example, that are particularly meaningful to the Hindu tradition, and no historical records on the order of Chinese classics such as the Book of History or the Spring and Autumn Annals. Nor are there powerful establishers like Gautama Buddha, Vardhamana Mahavira, or Guru Nanak, all of them historically grounded shapers and transmitters of traditions in South Asia outside Hinduism. Most of the usual textual, institutional, and biographical criteria are missing until fairly late in the stream of time.

Certain features do present themselves from the collective Indian experience, however, and it is these we may designate historical breaks in an overview. One of these is the emergence of full-scale urban societies along the Indus River, societies that formed the first cohesive civilization in South Asia in the third and second millennia BCE. A second is the appearance of the Vedas, providing a Vedic age, the period when these great oral traditions were dominant paradigms and unchallenged sacred utterances for large segments of the populace.

The third feature is also an oral-literary one, a period when new post-Vedic texts and accompanying traditions surfaced to establish the classical definitions of Hinduism. The earliest of these post-Vedic texts were oral compositions, like the Vedas, eventually transmitted into writing. The Dharma Shastras, such as the Laws of Manu employed in chapter one as a link midway between ancient Vedic Hinduism and medieval regional Hinduism, were among them. But the two most important post-Vedic works were the great Sanskrit epics, the *Mahabharata* and the *Ramayana.* These vast collections of verses became classical storehouses of Hindu mythology, folklore, and doctrine. So encompassing of tradition were these Sanskrit epics, and so thoroughly did they dominate cultural life in the first several centuries of the Common Era, this third period might well be labeled an epic age. Its last phase witnessed the growth of towns with temples that served as ceremonial centers for extensive areas of the subcontinent, regions that also embraced other pilgrimage goals focused on sacred mountains and rivers. These centers in turn generated still more texts and traditions, including the classical treatises of Yoga and other philosophical schools, additional collections of mythology known as "old stories" or Puranas, and esoteric texts known as Tantras that focused on special techniques for liberation. The final phase of this epic age also displayed the flowering of ancient Indian culture and its most creative genius in literature, music, the arts, and philosophy.

Finally, subsequent to this formation of classical Hinduism in a post-Vedic age, two additional periods can be identified as medieval and modern. In the fourth or medieval age—median, that is, between classical and modern—several forceful minds and personalities came to identify and synthesize the philosophical, theological, and devotional bases of the faith. Shankara and Ramanuja were the most significant voices of this age. From the sixth to the seventeenth centuries regional poet-saints grew immensely popular when they countered traditional Sanskrit by employing their local languages as the medium of devotional songs.

In the fifth or modern period Hinduism has undergone—and is undergoing—a series of comprehensive and affective reforms. Two particular challenges called for responses from the Hindu tradition during the last eight centuries. One of these, largely a feature of the medieval period, was the encounter with Islam as an intrusive and innovative cultural entity in South Asia. The other, largely a feature of the modern period that continues today, is the encounter with the political, religious, and cultural force of the West.

Thus we may examine five segments of the Hindu experience. A rough chronology and set of comparative time-lines might serve for the purposes of this overview:

The Indus Valley Civilization—c. 2500–1750 BCE

A Vedic Age—c. 1200–200 BCE

An Epic Age—c. 400 BCE–800 CE

Medieval South Asia—c. 750–1750 CE

Modern South Asia—c. 1750–the present

If these five periods are situated in rough millennia (thousand-year eras), something of their duration as well as overlap is seen in the context of South Asian history at large (see table 1).

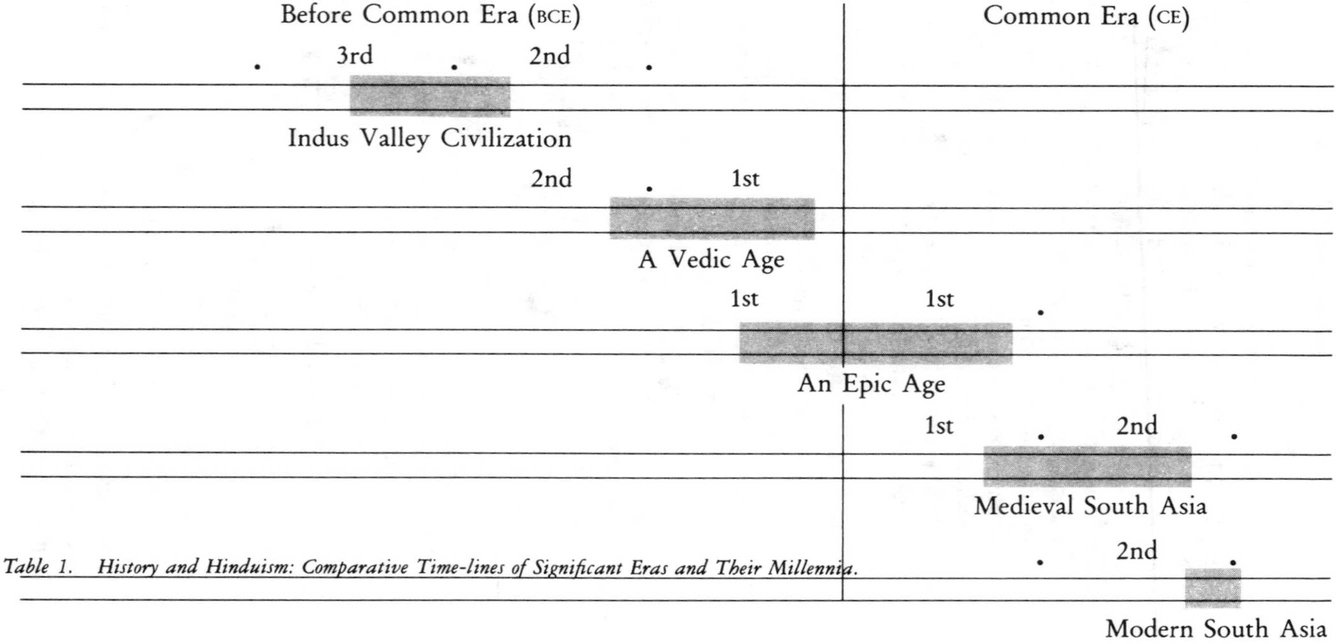

Before Common Era (BCE) | Common Era (CE)

3rd · 2nd

Indus Valley Civilization

2nd · 1st

A Vedic Age

1st | 1st

An Epic Age

1st · 2nd

Medieval South Asia

2nd

Modern South Asia

Table 1. History and Hinduism: Comparative Time-lines of Significant Eras and Their Millennia.

From the outsider's historical point of view, essential experiences and expressions have been mixed into the rich Hindu synthesis in each of these periods. From the insider's traditional point of view, however, the enduring features of Hinduism have remained unaltered by the flow of history, "time ripening," or any circumstance of linguistic, ethnic, social, or political change. The marvelous thing about the faith is that both of these seemingly contradictory points of view are true, each in its own way, and both must be heard by the student of Hinduism.

Important to remember, therefore, is that this segmentation of human experience into ages and periods, while familiar to Western experience, is largely absent from Hindu tradition. These divisions are a search for organization, chronology, continuity, and development. In chapters four and five we will look through and beyond these divisions in order to focus on interactive worldviews and the dynamics of Hinduism. By and large these take scant notice of our five periods, or any other schedule of historical episodes, even while their expressions are concrete evidence of cumulative memory and changing experience.

Earliest Civilization: The Indus Valley

The Indus, one of the world's greatest river systems, flows from southwestern Tibet 1,800 miles before it empties into the Arabian Sea. Its earliest known name is the Sanskrit—Sindhu—which provided through ancient Greek and Persian both "India" and "Hindu" as designations for the land beyond the river and its people. The northwest region of India, known as the Punjab ("land of five rivers"), takes its name from five large tributaries of the lower Indus. And now in our time the river has lent its name once again, for lack of an ancient one, to what appears to have been a coherent urban civilization, one that developed in the middle of the third millennium BCE and lasted for about eight centuries. A string of cities, the largest of them about one mile square, reached from Harappa on the Ravi tributary in the north down through Mohenjo-daro to Lothal in the delta on the sea.

This civilization resulted from the discovery of rich arable soil in the Indus flood plain (just as earlier urban societies developed

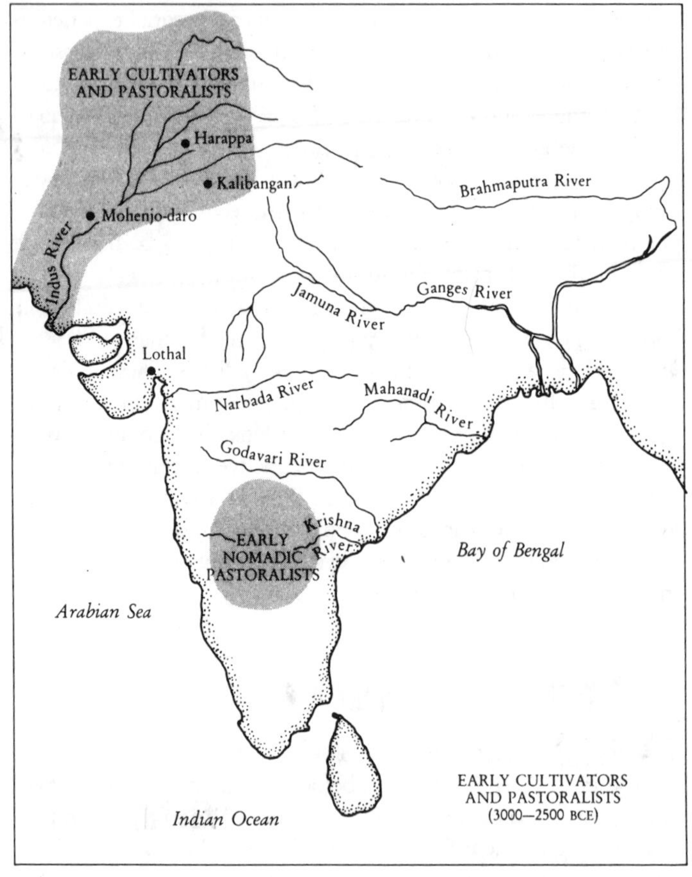

along the Nile and along the Tigris and Euphrates, and a later one on the alluvial plain of North China). Smaller, pre-Indus settlements can be traced by archaeologists back into the seventh millennium BCE in Baluchistan and Afghanistan. Those early settlers—seminomadic pastoralists, sedentary cultivators, and some who combined cattle herding with small-scale wheat-barley agriculture—provided a technological heritage many thousands of years old, one that blossomed dramatically when transferred eastward to the Indus River system in the third millennium BCE. About four thousand years ago the civilization may have been at full strength, with upwards of two hundred villages and towns and half a dozen cities, a common system of weights and measures, uniform building supplies and techniques, granary systems to store harvests, and established trade routes that aimed westward by sea into the Persian Gulf and northward by land into Central Asia.

From seventy years of archaeology a great deal has been learned about the material culture of the Indus sites. It is surprising therefore that the religious life remains largely hidden. One may only speculate. For starters, there are over two thousand brief inscriptions, and more coming to light every season, but scholars cannot agree on the reading of their signs. Second, the inscriptions are on a startling array of finely carved steatite stamp "seals," square or rectangular, about two inches wide, with what appear to be sacred figures of humans and animals in mythic and ritual scenes. But the myths and rituals are absent, and the "humans" could be deities, royalty, heroes, heroines, sacrificial victims, devotees. With about 400 graphemes and no decipherable inscription even the purpose of this seal-writing remains unknown. Third, there is nothing clearly identified as a shrine or a temple in any excavated site. If Mohenjo-daro or Harappa became established ceremonial centers for their regions, perhaps they resembled ancient Chinese cities more than the temple-centered urban societies of Egypt, Mesopotamia, and Anatolia in that they relied more on cosmic images and symbols than upon the building of impressive dwellings for deities.

Having stated how much information is lacking, we may proceed to some of the more useful speculations concerning religious life along the Indus River about 2000 BCE. We have the benefit of hindsight, of course, and often expect features of today's Hinduism to be at least four thousand years old. (A slide rule for students of South Asia, by the way, might be this: every aspect of life in the subcontinent is much older than it looks, except *this* one under investigation, which began in the summer of 1990.) It may be imprudent to second-guess a culture that left us, thus far, few clues concerning its social structure, few significant works of art or institutional architecture, no literature of any kind, and only a disputed supposition that its language or languages belonged to "Proto-Dravidian." (The Dravidian family is confined, as it is known historically, to four languages of South India and the remnant Brahui now spoken by a quarter of a million pastoralists in Pakistan.)

But second-guessing is an established academic tradition, a tantalizing one, and quite frequently instructive. If some of the peoples of Pakistan and northwestern India still today plow their fields in the patterns of ancient furrows or make wooden carts that resemble toy miniatures found in levels of Harappa, then perhaps something of their spiritual ethos may have survived four or five thousand years as well.

First, the overall impression from surveying the excavated Indus sites is one of urbanity, sophistication, well-being, ordered existence. From the huge wheat and barley storage systems down to the presence of household and public drainage works, there is visible an overarching hand of authority and urban planning. From the uniformity of material culture across hundreds of miles and a great many centuries there is felt the weight of tradition. It is not difficult to imagine a centralized religious authority corresponding to, or perhaps superseding, the obvious political and economic authority.

Second, if major cities such as Harappa, Mohenjo-daro, and Kalibangan did serve as ceremonial centers, several features in their

New excavations in the Harappa cemetery, 1987. (Photo by J. M. Kenoyer, courtesy of the University of California at Berkeley Project at Harappa, an ongoing project with the Department of Archaeology and Museums, Government of Pakistan.)

layouts are worth remarking on. They are axially oriented north-south with streets in a grid and raised, brick-walled mounds dominating the western quarter. Burials in cemeteries frequently also reveal a common north-south alignment, head to the north, a direction that remains to this day an auspicious one in South Asia. On top of Mohenjo-daro's mound, at the center, is a tank that archaeologists have labeled the "great bath." It has wide steps at each end and resembles the ritual bathing tanks of Hindu temples that began to appear in the subcontinent in the first few centuries CE. If there were constructions of steps descending into the river for ritual bathing, as is the case with every riverside town or city in India today, these have long since disappeared without a trace.

Third, as we might suspect from a long-established agrarian tradition, there appear to have been prominent feminine images and symbols in the deepest strata of the region, going back to the pre-urban seventh millennium. Small, distinctive terra-cotta females, of a popular, perhaps votive type, are abundant in village sites and common in the larger settlements. And many of the most intriguing motifs on the Indus civilization seals include feminine powers, frequently linked with symbols of vegetation or of animals, including real animals and composite or mythic creatures. After the Indus cities withered, nude female figurines maintained their importance in village cultures; later there were to appear the voluptuous lifesize figures, the *yakshi*s of classical Hinduism, Jainism, and Buddhism. And the presence of the tiger among the animals associated with females depicted on the seals reminds us again that tigers and lions were the favored mounts of later Hindu goddesses, and the goddess as lion or with lion, leopard, or panther was a familiar motif in ancient Egypt, the Aegean, Asia Minor, and the whole of West Asia.

Fourth, these animal symbols in their own right are graphically powerful expressions and immediately call to mind the significance of zoological symbols, both wild and domestic, in the history of Hinduism. With the exception of composite creatures and serpents, not easy to sex, the prominent animals are horned males—the bull, water buffalo, ram, and others. The buffalo (*bubalus*) and two distinct species of cattle, one the humped zebu (*bos indicus*) and the other a humpless relation to the *bos primigenius* of West Asia, had been domestic animals in South Asia for several thousand years. All three appear to have gained sacred status in pre-Indus religion, often in association with vegetation—the pipal tree or its leaves, to take one example.

Certain Indus seals and impressions show a humanlike male seated in "yogic" posture, wearing what may be a buffalo mask as well as buffalo horns, and surrounded by animals both wild and domestic. Mistakenly identified several decades ago as a "proto-**Shiva**," with reference to the later Vedic-Hindu god, this commanding and obviously significant figure seems now to be even older than the Indus civilization and may be related to a similar

Seal 420 from Mohenjo-daro, the most widely discussed object from the Indus Valley civilization. A horned animal–masked male figure of apparent cultic significance sits surrounded by a number of powerful wild animals. (National Museum, New Delhi)

figure from Elam, a more ancient culture to the west that was closely linked to adjacent Mesopotamian urban societies.

Perhaps this figure should be studied in connection with the goddess-and-male-consort known in West Asia. The comparative study of ancient urban cultures from the Danube to the Aegean area (Old European civilization) and from Anatolia across West Asia to Iran reveals a striking association: a timeless Great Goddess, who guarantees the fertility of plants, animals, and humans, is depicted either with or as trees or pillars, in sacred groves, with serpents, lions, and a wide variety of animals known for powers of regeneration. Her subordinate male consort, on the other hand, is frequently identified with the victim of blood sacrifice, a virile horned animal such as the bull, for example. It is the male of the pair who is subject to time via sacrificial death, sometimes dismemberment, and then regeneration at the hands of the goddess. Whether or not the Indus civilization based much or any of its religious traditions upon such a pairing, with the buffalo at times in the role of the bull (as suggested recently by one scholar), remains to be seen and will probably be known only from decipherment of the script.

At this point what is most exciting about the religion of the Indus in the third and second millennia BCE is not what we know but what we may be about to learn in the coming decades. Many of the essential features of this vaguely appreciated but decidedly formative era may at last be visible as studies in ethnoarchaeology, philology, and the history of religions converge on the material evidence brought out by new excavations and new technologies.

What caused the demise of the Indus urban civilization is at this point as mysterious as the Indus script and the subject of as many interpretations. About 1750 BCE declining standards in construction and the appearance of different types of pottery signal a break in the Indus time-line. Whether immigrations of new peoples, droughts, deforestation, floods, or alterations in the course of the life-giving river were causes or contributing factors cannot be determined from current evidence. In any case, while the great urban sites decayed, some village areas, particularly those to the east of the river, maintained their traditions for a time, although without benefit of the former great commercial and ceremonial centers and what must have been vivid cosmopolitan traffic. It is these areas to the east in the second half of the second millennium BCE that may well have served as links to preserve and disperse age-old Indus traditions.

Nowhere else on the subcontinent were there urban complexes to rival the Indus cities, but other cultures did leave their traces. For example, in the Deccan of South India there were seminomadic pastoralists who penned their cattle in large corrals and quartered themselves within similar stockades. These structures were burned periodically, perhaps at the times of seasonal grazing migrations, leaving behind distinctive cow-dung ash-mounds that date from c. 3000 BCE on. The notion of a cattle pen associated not only with human sustenance but also with kinship, that is, the connected human generations, may indeed be very old in India, and possibly multicultural. In later Hinduism an individual's *gotra* or clan-descent is an important aspect of identity; the Sanskrit word literally means "cow pen."

Other early cultures of North and peninsular India are known from their surviving pottery; their stone tools or metalworking in copper, bronze, or gold; and their agrarian or pastoral means of subsistence. Once again, little is known of religious life, but certain phenomena are recurrent in widely separated sites: the long-horned humped bull, either in terra-cotta figurines or in rock art; distinctive female figurines, thought to be popular goddesses; burials and grave-goods, sometimes in urns beneath the floors of dwellings or between them. Other artifacts are unique: a copper anthropomorph, possibly for ritual use, and a remarkable find of large animals cast in solid copper—a rhino and a water buffalo, each on axled wheels; an elephant on a pedestal fashioned to hold wheels; and a rider on a light two-wheeled chariot behind two yoked oxen, all from the second half of the second millennium BCE.

The contributions to the growth of Hinduism of these bygone cultures, their responses to the sacred in the symbols of animals, plants, rivers, earth, fire, and the other elements can only be the subject of speculation, since they left us no inscriptions, literature, or sacred architecture. We know only from the literatures of invading peoples who later encountered and generally subjugated them that the newcomers themselves were gradually and indelibly transformed in major and minor ways by a vivid new religious pluralism and had to devise means of separating, incorporating, or explaining alternate worldviews, rituals, beliefs, and practices.

A Vedic Age

> With the sacrifice the gods sacrificed to the sacrifice. . . . These were the first cosmic laws.
>
> *Rigveda* 10.90.16 (concluding verse of the hymn of Purusha)

Returning to the upper Indus in the northwestern area of the subcontinent, we confront one of the major intrigues of South Asian history. In the same early centuries of the second millennium BCE as the decline and demise of the Indus cities there arrived new peoples whose dynamic religious expressions structured ancient Hinduism for more than a thousand years. These people—or peoples more precisely, since they probably arrived in serial migrations that lasted for many centuries—were nomadic pastoralists from Central Asia and the Iranian plateau entering the subcontinent through passes in the mountains of what is now Afghanistan and Pakistan. They spoke dialects of a language descended from Proto–Indo-European speech current perhaps two or three thousand years earlier.

Comparative religious studies and linguistics, with recent assistance from archaeology, have permitted speculation about the worldview and symbol system of the Proto–Indo-Europeans who may have inhabited the lower valleys of the Ural, the Volga, and the Don where these rivers reached the Caspian and the Black seas. These cattle and horse herders supplemented a pastoral economy with limited agriculture in the fifth millennium BCE—almost seven thousand years ago—before their Eurasian dispersal to the west, east, and south to establish regional languages and cultures from Iceland to India.

One great set of migrations eastward into Central Asia was the Indo-Iranian one, so called because a split occurred, perhaps some time after 2000 BCE, between those peoples who moved with their herds south and then westward onto the Iranian plateau and those Indo-Aryan speakers who negotiated high mountain passes to cross over into India. Eventually these two separated nomadic groups composed religious poetry as the earliest literature of all the migrant Indo-Europeans. Comparative studies of the ancient Indian Vedas with the scarcer remnants of ancient Iranian texts—the Avesta—indicate that religious traditions in these two distinct areas of Asia appear to have developed along parallel lines for some centuries after the division. Basic mythologies, community and domestic rituals, social classes, priestly functions—even the nomenclature of myth and cult—are illuminative one of the other, and many key names and terms are cognate.

Eventually, however, the religious reforms of Zarathustra and others in Iran yielded a major new religion, Zoroastrianism, about the same time that India produced a set of remarkable philosophers who transformed the religion of ancient Vedic Hinduism into classical Hinduism. After that, Indo-Iranian parallelism continued only in echoes from the distant past, for example in the perpetuation of mythic themes in long, oral epics about ancient heroes and kings. A remarkable event more than a thousand years later, however, allowed Zoroastrian refugees from medieval Islamic persecutions in Iran to migrate to western India. Today, bracketed by their ancient cousins, descendants of these refugees live as Parsis ("Persians") in the land of the Hindus.

The degree of contact between waves of Indo-Aryan nomads and the settled cultivators and herders of the Indus cities is the subject of considerable speculation. Early Vedic literature celebrates repeated conquests of forts, including those labeled "triple forts," but describes nothing like the cities of the archaeological record. It is possible that the migrants who produced Vedic poetry, ritual, and speculation were but one of several Indo-Aryan speaking cultures mobile in the second millennium BCE. In any event, they were the ones who impressed and altered South Asian history with their formidable culture.

The Vedas

The Vedic religion of ancient India takes its name from, and is dependent upon, the Vedas, books of "knowledge" (*veda*). As already noted, these oral texts, regarded as unitary and eternal, are understood to have no human or divine origin. They have always been a sacred sound, **brahman**, a foundational cosmic utterance.

Somehow it was intuited by ancient seers, the *rishis*, an aggregate of seven sages who then transmitted the Vedas for the benefit of the world. The **mantras** or verse formulas of the Vedas always had and still have today an aural destiny. Buddhist canonical texts were committed to writing in India late in the first century BCE, but many centuries later, when portions of some Vedas were written on birch bark or palm leaves or eventually printed on paper by European scholars, they were still learned by hearing and expressed by recitation. The whole corpus of Vedic texts is known as **shruti**, what is heard, since those who transmit it from generation to generation learn the mantras a lesson at a time by listening. This unitary revelation is thus a sacred verbal power employed in one or another liturgical composition—such as an invocation, a hymn in praise of a deity, a directive for an offering—in the entire ritual system that structures Vedic religion.

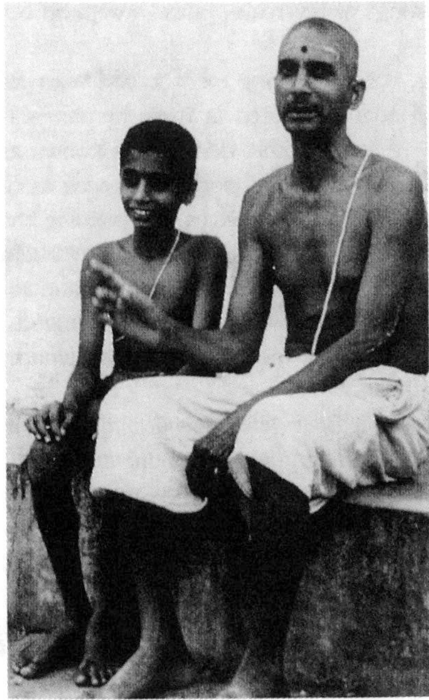

Learning to recite, phrase by phrase, from a portion of the Vedic oral tradition. This boy will spend eight or more years committing to memory a particular branch of the Vedas. If capable he will then go on to another branch for several more years.

This vast body of *shruti* included in antiquity as many as several scores of separate texts. Over the centuries many were lost, but the extant corpus is still enormous, with some of the survivors reaching more than a thousand pages each in contemporary printed editions. From the nontraditional, text-critical point of view this corpus is a series of genres that required a full millennium to complete. It extended from the four early collections known as Samhitas—the *Rigveda*, *Yajurveda*, *Samaveda*, and *Atharvaveda*, all composed between about 1200 BCE and 900 BCE—down through genres known as Brahmanas and Aranyakas to the last of the Upanishads and ritual Sutras about 200 BCE. Let us examine briefly each of these Vedic literary assemblies, keeping always in mind their nature as oral texts.

First and foremost of the Samhitas (and of all the Vedas) is the *Rigveda*. It is a large hymnal, a collection of 1,028 metrical hymns to all the deities revered in the late second millennium BCE. **Indra**, **Varuna**, **Agni**, **Soma**, the **Ashvin** twins, **Vayu**, **Rudra** and **Vishnu** are among the many whose basic mythologies can be pieced together from these songs of reverence, praise, awe, and occasionally fear.

Indra, the hard-drinking, chariot-driving warrior god with an invincible thunderbolt weapon, is celebrated in more hymns—almost a quarter of the total—than any other deity. He is known as a heroic conqueror of enemies of the Vedic nomads, as well as of assorted demons, including the infamous **Vritra**. By piercing the belly of Vritra—a powerful cloud-serpent being who had withheld the life-giving waters and light—Indra released the rains and allowed creation to resume. As patron of warriors, king of the gods, and drinker of the sacred juice of *soma*, Indra has the most dynamic personality of all the pantheon.

Varuna is guardian of cosmic order (**rita**, a word replaced in later texts by *dharma*). Also a sovereign deity, he is universal monarch by virtue of his transcendent character as a sky god. Since he is known to discipline those who break his cosmic laws, many hymns address him in petitions for mercy and hopes that he will not inflict disease as a punishment. Frequently this god of occult powers is invoked together with Mitra, another ancient celestial deity, and one who is a protective, mediating figure.

Agni is the mysterious sacred fire, at once the sacrificial element and the interior energy of the universe and each of its beings. Known for his multiple births, he is resident in all three levels of the cosmos. Agni is addressed in the opening verse of the *Rigveda*, and as both primordial sacrificer and fulfiller of every priestly function he is the oblation-bearer to the gods and the divine messenger to humans. The hidden, covert, secret nature of Agni is a constant reference in the *mantra*s. He is lord of every household (in the hearth), eater of corpses (in the cremation pyre), born anew every day (from the kindling sticks), and yet omniscient (as fire in the sun, lightning, waters, and plants).

Soma is, like Agni, simultaneously substance and mystery. Plant, juice, king, sacrificial victim, and god are among the roles assigned by Vedic faith to this being. Stolen from the highest heaven by an eagle, the plant and its essence (ritually pressed juice) bestow upon the divine or priestly drinkers both poetic insight and immortality. Indra, the warrior deity, becomes invincible in battle through soma-intoxication, while the ecstasy of poets allows them supernatural vision.

The Ashvin twins are a good example of pastoral deities. Identified as horsemen, they are celestial charioteers, an auspicious sight in the early dawn behind their golden chariot. Connected with the fertility of herds, crops, and humans, they are also healers of diseases and rescuers of those in danger.

Vayu was the first of the gods to drink soma. Closely associated with Indra, Vayu is a god of wind and warfare, and one also connected with fate and cults of the dead.

Rudra is an outsider god, a howler (as his name implies) in the wilderness. More paradoxical and unpredictable than "insider" deities, he may either burn with his fierce heat of destruction or heal with his cooling remedies. His sons are a collection of storm deities known either as the **Maruts** or the Rudras. Euphemistically called Shiva, "auspicious," in later literature, he lives on in classical Hinduism as one of the two major male deities.

Vishnu is the other preeminent male deity of classical Hinduism; like Rudra, he is a relatively minor figure in the *Rigveda*. The god who crosses the universe in three great strides, Vishnu is sometimes involved in Indra's exploits.

Without much further detail it is worth noting that our knowledge of some of these deities and their cults is more or less enhanced by comparative Indo-Iranian and Indo-European studies. The mythology and cult of *haoma* in ancient Iran, for example, reveals multiple parallels to the Vedic *soma* tradition. The Ashvins have their mythological counterpart twins in the Dioskouroi of ancient Greece and Gemini of ancient Rome, as Yama (whose name in fact means "twin") has a match in the Iranian Yima. One of Indra's correlates is Thor, the hard-drinking, chariot-driving warrior deity of ancient Scandinavia.

There are scores of other gods and collective powers addressed or extolled in the *Rigveda*. Surya and Savitr are solar gods, Yama is a primal being who is the first to die and therefore lord of the dead, and Pushan, another pastoral deity, is patron of travelers and a bringer of prosperity. Although there are numerous feminine powers in the *Rigveda*, some of them connected in a vague and shadowy way with fate and destiny, the pantheon had few places of prominence for goddesses. **Ushas** is the dawn, celebrated by the poets for her splendor. **Aditi**, the primordial "boundless" goddess, is mother of a class of sovereign deities, including Varuna. And **Sarasvati**, associated with the ancient river of that name, has functions similar to those of the Ashvins.

Turning now to the three later Samhitas—the *Yajurveda*, *Samaveda*, and *Atharvaveda*—mantras from the *Rigveda* were employed in all three of these collections. Specific purposes were in mind, and certain modifications or additions to the Rigvedic text were performed, including in some cases prose additions. The *Yajurveda* became a manual of directions for the performance of sacrifices and included the mantra formulas chanted in them. The *Samaveda*, an index to melodies required in the great *soma* sacrifices, set specific mantras to a seven-note musical scale. The last Samhita, the *Atharvaveda*, not concerned with the priestly sacrificial system, drew together certain domestic rituals and the religious concerns of popular culture, including charms, spells, incantations, and India's earliest medical and pharmacological lore.

From two to five branches of each of these Samhitas survive today. In antiquity each of them generated discourses about the procedures of the sacrifices and the meanings attributed to them. Such traditions when assembled as oral texts were called Brahmanas, and they were followed by other texts known as "forest books" or Aranyakas, with both of these commentarial genres fully developed about 1000 BCE to 700 BCE. By 800 BCE certain directives for each of the great sacrifices began to appear, and these were assembled and edited as ritual manuals known as Shrauta Sutras (**shrauta**, concerned with **shruti**). And by 600 BCE still another genre surfaced, this one philosophical, esoteric, and radical in its substitution of knowledge of the eternal Self for knowledge of the sacrifice.

To take an example from this confusing array of texts within branches, schools, and genres of the Vedas, consider the Brahman boy in the photo on page 27. He was born into the Taittiriya branch of the Black Yajurveda, so he must begin his Vedic instruction by learning a set sequence of Taittiriya texts: the *Taittiriya Samhita*, *Taittiriya Brahmana*, *Taittiriya Aranyaka*, *Taittiriya Upanishad*, and the *Apastamba Shrauta Sutra*, a kind of handbook of the great sacrifices of the Taittiriyins. This will require some eight to twelve years of daily effort on his part. If he is successful in his examinations he may then begin another Samhita, the *Rigveda*, for example, and proceed with it daily, followed by the *Aitareya Brahmana*, and so on to the *Ashvalayana Shrauta Sutra*. If his memory is sufficiently agile his instructor or **guru** will also train him to recite portions of the same text in recitation patterns far more complicated than the direct word-by-word order with which he begins.

As an illustration of the relationship of these texts and the way in which this boy may learn them, table 2 provides a structure for just two of the four Samhitas and their total of eleven branches.

Table 2. The Sequence of Texts in Two Branches of the Vedas.

	Yajurveda:	*Rigveda:*
Samhita	Taittiriya branch	Shakala branch
Brahmana	Taittiriya	Aitareya
Aranyaka	Taittiriya	Aitareya
Upanishad	Taittiriya	Aitareya
Ritual Sutra	Apastamba	Ashvalayana

There is much more to "the Vedas" than this brief discussion allows. Other components of Vedic and related post-Vedic textual traditions will be discussed further under the rubric of the worldview and the systematic ritual.

The Early Vedic Worldview

In order to understand the significance of the Vedas and Vedic Hinduism several related concepts are worth reviewing. One might say that the seeds of each were carried into South Asia with the migrant Indo-Aryans and then planted and nurtured in the specific soil and climate of India, that is to say in the territory of the Indus and the Ganges rivers where indigenous religious traditions had long been fertile.

These related notions are the following: First, the universe is a projection of a primordially sacrificed body of a cosmic being. The myth of this cosmic Self, **Purusha** (literally, "man, person"), who is also known in later Vedic texts as **Prajapati**, Lord of creatures, is a primary creation myth.

Second, it is a human responsibility to refabricate and sacrifice anew that cosmic body. This is a continuous process that regenerates the world through human spiritual knowledge and effort (*karma*). The myth of Purusha announces what was done in the beginning; the ritual accomplished by the priests assumes responsibility for a continuing world.

And third, there are two mysterious cosmic substances—fire and plant—that must be identified and made available through ritual work. One, Agni, pervasive sacred fire, is life maintaining and reveals sustaining correspondences between cosmic and human energies. The other, Soma, immortal sacred plant, is life transcending and reveals visions to humans of the other world, the realm that is not created and therefore is not subject to change.

These three concepts structured a faith that endured in South Asia for over a thousand years until the unveiling of new spiritual emphases in the classical Hinduism of a post-Vedic age. A few significant details of each of these notions might be pursued here; and because this early Vedic worldview is foundational, later chapters will expand upon them further.

First, existence is understood as a process of projection and assimilation. There is unity in the macrocosm (the world of the unmanifest) and multiplicity in the microcosm (creation, the world of phenomena). Each, however, is divided in three parts, each is hierarchic (that is, the three parts are ranked one above another in authority and power), and each is organically interdependent (that is, the parts work together as one being with three separate functions). It is an extraordinary system, at once tidy and complex. For example, an individual human body has three components (identified later in the classical medical literature as *dosha*s, humors), the human social body has three echelons (identified as **varnas**, "colors" or classes), and the world itself has three characteristics (identified later in the philosophical texts as **gunas**, "threads" or qualities)—all because these layered bodies are replications of the divine tripartite cosmic being. The process of projection and assimilation, of creation and reintegration is a continuously sacrificial one. The world in its multiple forms, human society with its varied classes, and an individual with diverse bodily parts are all the result of the sacrifice and dismemberment of an original unity, the sacrifice Being, just as the death of a world or an individual is an assimilation—by sacrifice—of multiple parts back into the tripartite whole.[1]

The Purusha hymn cited at the head of this segment, *Rigveda* 10.90, is the oldest documentation for such an Indo-European sacrificial cosmogony. And Vedic texts subsequent to the *Rigveda* continue to authenticate these correspondences of the upper three social classes and the individual sacrificer with the householder's three-fire ritual system and the return of a sacrificer at death—by means of his three fires—to the three-level cosmos. Table 3 portrays the continuity of such projection and assimilation.

A second imported concept concerns human responsibility for this continuous sacrificial process. Since the projected world is a result of a divine sacrifice (**yajna**), the continued existence of the world is dependent on repetitions of that primordial, cosmogonic event. As the Purusha hymn declares, the original cosmic laws were laid down by sacrifice. Once created, the world is thus constantly re-created by sacrifice. But now the ritual action is accomplished by human agents, namely the godlike Brahmans who take

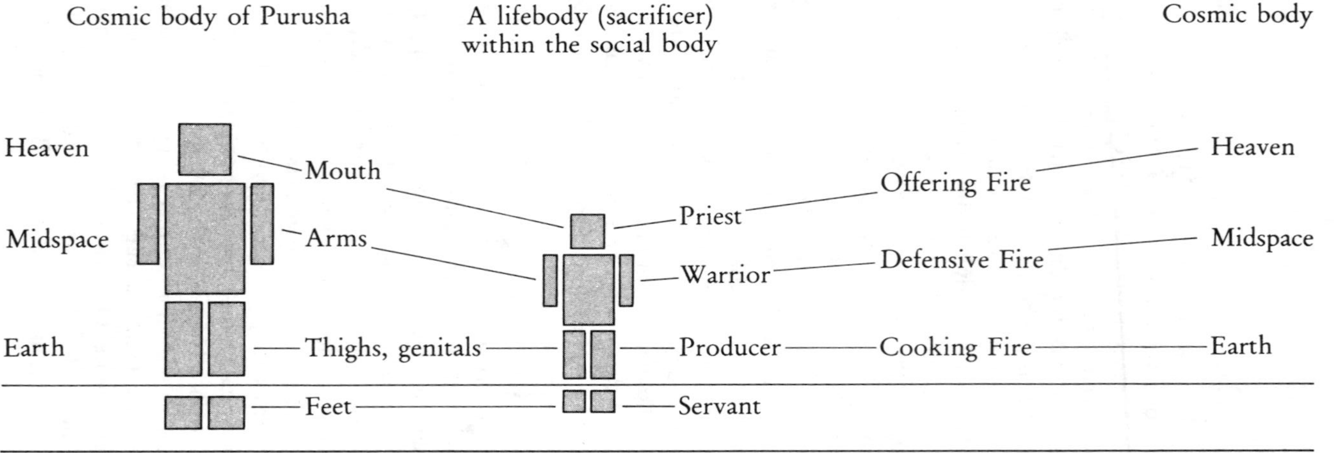

*Table 3. The Continuous Vedic Sacrifice**

*A lifebody, like the social body of four classes and the householder's system of three fires, is first a projection from the cosmic body of Purusha, then an assimilation back into the cosmic body. (The servant class, like the feet of Purusha, is subordinate and outside the ritual system that —like the cosmos—must be tripartite.)

upon themselves the work of the deities. The sovereign power of the priestly Brahman class becomes apparent in two astounding tasks: Brahmans, not gods, perpetuate the eternal sacred utterance, *brahman*, in the form of *mantra*s that are, in their totality, *veda*, sacred knowledge. And Brahmans, not gods, perpetuate the world through sacrifice. This sacrifice or ritual work (*karma*) proceeds on two separate but interactive scales. One is the communal, *shrauta*, world-regenerating schedule with staffs of as many as sixteen or seventeen priests. The other is a familial, domestic (**grihya**) one accomplished by the householder with or without a family priest. Each of the Vedic schools transmitted Sutras for both of these schedules of sacrifice, the Grihya Sutras in general later than, and similar in outline to, the Shrauta Sutras.

For example, with reference to table 3, procedures for the cremation of a deceased householder-sacrificer are described in the *Shankhayana Shrauta Sutra* of the Kaushitaki branch of the *Rig-veda*. His offering fire is placed at his head, his southern fire on his right side, his cooking fire close to his belly and genitals, his two fire sticks on his thighs, and the entire body is thus returned by the god Agni, the sacred fire, to the threefold cosmos as a "last sacrifice." Such an offering is accomplished by his oldest son as new and continuing householder-sacrificer.

The third Indo-European concept brought into India some 3,500 years ago involves an interaction of both myth and cult focused on concepts of sacred fire and sacred plant. There is a life-maintaining fire that pervades all and translates mutable existence to immutability, and there is a life-transcending plant of celestial origin that provides mortals with poetic inspiration and immortality. Like Purusha these two substances are divisible, macro-microcosmic, and obtainable by the ritual use of a special knowledge, that of operational correspondences between the divine/human and the unmanifest/manifest realms. As noted in the survey of Vedic deities, Agni is the god within the sacred element of fire, resident in every household and in the body of every living creature. Nomadic pastoralists of the late second millennium BCE attached special importance to constructing settlements with hearths. Vedic texts emphasize repeatedly the notion of being grounded, established, connected by assembling a hearth, by situating Agni. The significance of course transcended any economic concern or architectural detail regarding the transport of fire. What is established by a sacred presence is the self within the family within the community within the cosmos, and the constructive event is again an echo of the original sacrifice, the original creative event. As the Vedic poet-philosophers elaborated their doctrine of sacrifice, Agni became identified with Purusha-Prajapati and thereby with the transcendent self of the sacrificer. Fashioning the simplest domestic hearth or the year-long construction of a gigantic fireplace of 10,800 enormous bricks was necessary ritual work, an integrative cosmogonic act.

As for the cult of a divine plant, an elaborate sacred drama was already in place, probably for many centuries, among the Indo-Iranian nomadic pastoralists. Their descendants perpetuated this sacred drama that focused on *soma* in India and *haoma* in Iran. Acquisition of the plant from mountain tribal peoples, proceeding with this *soma* on a special cart onto the sacred field of fire, its royal enthronement, ritual immolation along with one or more animal victims, then pressing to obtain the elixirlike and probably hallucinogenic juice—all these and other ritual stages preceded the offering to the gods and the priestly sharing of this sacred essence. This drama of transformation became the focal point of institutional Vedic religion, as it remains to this day among the tiny remnant of authentic Vedic Brahman communities in South India. Both fire and plant were therefore simultaneously gods and divine substances that could be collected through the combined spiritual technology and physical labor of Brahman priests acting as agents in the necessary work of sacrifice and world-maintenance. In the great synthesizing text known as the Brahmana-of-the-hundred-paths, the *Shatapatha Brahmana*, these two, Agni and Soma, were brought together as principals in the cosmic mystery of the fire altar.

Thus three notions—the universe defined as a projection of the primordially sacrificed body of Purusha, the application of precise spiritual technique in the great work (*karma*) of renewing worldly life from cosmic resources, and the identification of sacred fire and plant as liaisons in the sacrificial scheme of transcendent time and space—became the ground structure for a thousand-year tradition that was dominant in South Asia until the appearance of post-Vedic classical Hinduism.

A Systematic Ritual

As noted above, the Vedic sacrificer maintained his household system for both routine and extraordinary rituals. In the full-blown domestic schedule as described in the Grihya Sutras, a single fire received the dawn and evening twilight milk libations known as the *agnihotra* (oblation to Agni), or the offering known as *ishti* of grain cakes or butter porridge and milk, or the fortnightly offerings on the days of the new and full moon. Particularly important were offerings made to the ancestors on the new-moon day succeeding the "dark" or waning moon fortnight of each lunar month, since the dead required sustenance on a regular basis from their living descendants. At the outset of three significant cosmic transitions—the seasons of spring, rains, and autumn—there were "four-month" sacrifices. Aside from such daily, fortnightly, and seasonal schedules certain other rituals were occasional. The animal sacrifice, for example, included optional versions. The arrival of a special guest might call for the slaughter of a cow or goat, for example, to feast the visitor after invocation and feasting on the part of the gods, or meat as well as rice, grain cakes, and vegetables might be offered in the dark halves of three successive months to nourish the ancestors.

An entirely personal schedule of rituals concerned the life cycle of every family member. Marriage, including the ritual conception of a new offspring as the final act of the wedding ceremony, rituals for the production of a male child and for safe delivery, birth of an infant, its naming ceremony and first feeding with solid food some months later, the child's first tonsure, thread-investiture in youth as initiation into Vedic texts and sacrifices, the opening and closing of instructional terms for the Vedic student as well as his ritual bath at the conclusion of study, cremation of the dead, and offerings to the ancestors (**shraddha**) in the form of rice balls (*pinda*)—all of these were important rites of passage occurring in the household. A **purohita** or domestic priest could be employed for many or all of these, but in most cases the male head of the household could act as the family's priest. Essential in all things ritual was the participation of the householder's wife, although the *mantra* recitations and most of the offerings were the husband's obligation.

All of these rituals served the household in the domestic scheme outlined in the Grihya Sutras. A magnified scale of sacrifice existed for those who aspired to a system governed by the Shrauta Sutras. The *soma* tradition, the most advanced of all *shrauta* rituals, called for a priestly staff divided not only by specialized functions but by texts as well. Four major priests were responsible for the four Vedic Samhitas. The *hota* or invoking priest recited from the *Rigveda*, the *adhvaryu* or executive priest directed the entire sacrifice and proclaimed from a recension of the *Yajurveda*, the *udgata* or chanting priest sang from the *Samaveda*, and finally, transcending this trio the *brahmán* or supervisory priest, possessing skillful knowledge (*vidya*) of all four Vedas, silently audited and surveyed the entire drama. Each of the four could employ three assistants for designated functions, a full staff thus being sixteen (occasionally seventeen for special rituals requiring an additional acolyte for the *brahmán*).

The power and scope of the Vedic *shrauta* ritual enterprise, one of the most complex known in the history of religions, is not easy to grasp. At its very heart is the creative murder known as sacrifice, that is to say, the ritually controlled violence done to the divine Soma and the animal victims following the pattern of Purusha-Prajapati's self-inflicted violence. Death, dismemberment, and dispersal are one side, regeneration, reintegration, and transcendence the other, all reflective in the continuity of sacrifice. The whole elaborate structure is cemented by the notion of ritual control.

Only a married householder skilled in *mantras* could extend his single household fire into the three sacred fires for the *shrauta* schedule (the offering, defensive, and cooking fires in table 3). The *agnyadheya* ritual established a three-fire domestic hearth employed for many of the same calendrical and other rituals accomplished in the one-fire domestic schedule, although on a grander scale of preparations, offerings, and *mantras*.

But the highest aspiration of the *ahitagni*, the householder maintaining three fires, was the *soma* sacrifice. The *agnishtoma*, a five-day ritual with three separate *soma*-pressing ceremonies on one day, was always the initial *soma* rite, and for most remained the pinnacle of religious life. The sacrificer (*yajamana*) underwent a period of consecration (*diksha*) in order to be eligible for the role of *soma* and animal offerer. Six other great *soma* rituals lay beyond the *agnishtoma*, with many variations regarding the number of *soma*-pressing days and the number and types of animal victims. Among the greatest of *shrauta* rituals were the *agnichayana* (the piling of the fire-altar in five layers of a thousand or more huge bricks, often in the form of the eagle who stole *soma* stalks from heaven), and the *vajapeya* (the *soma*-drink of power, with its emphasis on Prajapati's sacred number, seventeen). Some were royal sacrifices, such as the *rajasuya* or consecration of a king, involving chariot races, enthronement, and symbolic dice games, and the famous horse sacrifice, the *ashvamedha*.

The last named, with comparative evidence from the ancient Celtic, Roman, and Scythian horse sacrifices, was a sacrifice performed (rarely) by kings in India up until the seventeenth century CE. A successful performance of this demonstration of universal kingship required two years, the assembly of nearly seven hundred animals, a cast of four hundred warriors and four hundred women, and a virtual king's ransom in cows, land, and gold. The monarch as sacrificer was identified with the stallion-victim—who was permitted to wander freely for a year of territorial conquest—as well as with Purusha-Prajapati as the year and the world as newly integrated "king-dom." The smothering of the horse and channeling of its vital breath (prana) into the queen in symbolic sexual union was the climax of the rite on the middle of three *soma*-pressing days, and the expected fruition of this creative murder of the horse/king was of course a prince, a new king for the new kingdom.

Bound up in all the complexity of ritual activity on both major and minor scales was the fluid cosmic/human power of fire and plant, Agni as life maintaining, and Soma as life transcending. The mysterious entity known as sacrifice itself—identified with the elusive being of Purusha-Prajapati—expresses a simultaneity of life-maintenance and life-transcendence. Congruent with the regeneration of the entire world-as-it-is occurs the promotion of a single lifebody, the sacrificer, to life-as-it-might-be. That is to say, the individual accomplishing the ritual becomes "immortal," no longer material for assimilation and reprojection. In the synchronous mystery of sacrifice a solitary individual becomes destined to return to the unmanifest not to die, while the unitary world at large becomes destined to die precisely because it has been created all over again.

Obviously such notions, developing in multiple schools over centuries of time in the several regions of India, allowed for generous increments of speculation on human and world destiny. The concept of world-abandonment or renunciation was certainly among those speculations. A significant moment in Vedic rituals was designated **tyaga,** "abandonment," a turning over to the invited deities not only the offered substance, but the fruits or benefits of the ritual itself.

A Three-plus-One Society

Already remarked is the triadic principle of ordering in the Vedic worldview, one inherited from an apparent Proto–Indo-European threefold hierarchy of functions—priestly, warrior, and productive. The created universe, eternal Vedas, ranks of the gods, ritual fires, priesthood, and classes of human society are all tripartite and hierarchic according to function. With reference again to table 3 it may be seen that the three twiceborn classes—Brahmanas, Kshatriyas, and Vaishyas—are derived respectively from the mouth, arms, and thighs of Purusha. The Shudras, a subordinate fourth estate, are outside this triadic, interdependent society, excluded from both *mantras* and rituals, cosmically destined to serve the upper classes.

The notion of a subordinate fourth that "doesn't count" is an important one and is already there in the multivocal Purusha mythology. Three quarters of Purusha remain unmanifest during his sacrificial self-distribution; only one quarter becomes manifest in the created world. It is a way of saying that Purusha (Supreme Being, *Brahman*, the absolute) remains whole and undiminished by the act of creation, a way of expressing simultaneous transcendence and immanence of divinity. But it also says that this created world "doesn't count."

The essential triadic nature of the unmanifest and manifest worlds continues to be maintained by Vedic Hindu ritualists and philosophers, even when the symbol system becomes quite busy with variant numerologies. Fabrication of the Vedic fire altar in the *agnichayana* proceeds with five layers of bricks representing five levels of the world and the surrounding matrix, the body, of the constructed **atman** of the sacrificer. The interior triad, however, remains its skeleton. Still later there are expansions of the hierarchy to seven and nine, but the basic triad remains in play. It is a three-plus-other numerology. In the next chapter some of these later themes will be discussed further as Hindu expressions of classifying the universe.

For now it is important to consider the basic four *varnas* and the three-plus-other society first represented in the late *Rigveda* and assumed to be normative throughout the Vedic age. Brahmanas, responsible for the transmission and application of *mantras*, the directing of *yajnas*, and acceptance of those gifts (*dakshinas*) that provide ritual closure to sacrifices, were the dominant *varna*. Rajanyas or Kshatriyas, whose *dharma*, like that of their patron deity, Indra, was defense of the populace against enemies and demons, were the median rank. The warrior class was also the source of political sovereignty, namely kingship. And Vaishyas, the bulk of society, were those responsible for animal husbandry, agriculture, crafts, and trade, all of the activities that comprise the *dharma* of productivity.

In the course of their migrations across North India, Indo-Aryans encountered hundreds of varied indigenous societies. Many were subjugated or embraced as a part of Vedic civilization, added on at the bottom of the social scale under the rubric of Shudra. By the middle of the first millennium BCE, when the Upanishads and ritual Sutras were concluding genres of Vedic textual activity, Vedic civilization was no longer the simple three-plus-other *varna* system. There were powerful occupational guilds (*shrenis*) with significant impacts in social ranking. Many of the most essential artisans, as well as the great pool of agriculturalists, came from the Shudra class. There were elaborate strictures regarding ritual purity and impurity, and certain activities considered to be defiling were designated for communities who were then by definition unclean. The "other" *varna*, the Shudras, were broadly divided into those who were an actual component of society and those who were literally outside, a fifth class, later to be labeled Untouchables or outcastes (today's "Scheduled Castes").

By the time of the Dharma Sutras and Dharma Shastras in the last three centuries of the first millennium BCE these codes of law (*dharma*) were forced to explain how scores of separate communities (jatis, kinds of "birth") had come about. A traditional explanation was the mixing or confusion of *varnas*, that is, improper marriages between the original four classes. Thus the *dharma* of class came to be applied more rigidly in the post-Vedic period to the hierarchy of scores of separate communities (today known as castes[2]), separated by sacred laws that prohibit intermarriage and interdining. Appearing in the next segment of this chapter will be the Upanishadic formulation of the doctrine of rebirth, still another factor added to the many explanations for the variations and apparent inequities within human society, and the relative ranking of humans within the larger company of gods, animals, and demons.

The Upanishads and a New Worldview

Most of the Vedic branches or schools included in their chains of texts a genre of "forest books," Aranyakas, and short prose or verse works concerning mystical "correspondences," Upanishads. Some schools edited these texts as fused versions: the *Shatapatha Brahmana*, for example, concludes with an Upanishad known as the *Brihad* (Great) *Aranyaka*, one of the most important of all late Vedic texts. The "forest" denoted territory outside the village, private space where esoteric, hidden doctrines could be revealed to each new student. More than a dozen of these Vedic Upanishads evolved over a period of several centuries from about the eighth century BCE. Together they constituted a reformation—a reassessment of the sacrificial worldview and a redirection of religious energies inward toward salvation by insight and knowledge rather than reliance upon ritual action alone.

Their significance extended far beyond the Vedic tradition. This new vision, enlarged by non-Brahman as well as Brahman transmission, and linked with energetic ascetic movements (the **shramanas**, wandering renunciants) and the ideologies and techniques of salvation known later in the schools of Yoga and Samkhya, were crucial in the formation of new religious communities such as the Jainas, Buddhists, and Ajivikas. The flow of speculation in the period of the Brahmanas, Aranyakas, and Upanishads culminated in a radical new interpretation of sacrifice and its consequences; and because this interpretation forced clarification of the doctrines of *samsara* and *karma*, the Upanishads became a watershed for South Asian thought. In the final centuries of the first millennium BCE there was for the first time in South Asia a clear and distinct plurality of religious traditions, each with texts, doctrines, and institutions. What was to become "classic" and enduring in Hinduism emerged from gifted poet-philosophers in a four-hundred-year period of Upanishadic inspiration.

The point of departure for the Aranyakas and Upanishads remained the sacrifice, just as previously in the *Yajurveda* and *Samaveda* Samhitas and all the Brahmanas. The *Brihadaranyaka Upanishad*, for example, begins with an accounting of the parts of the *ashvamedha* sacrificial horse and their cosmic correspondences (eye=sun, breath=wind, and so forth), an indexing reminiscent of the notion of bodily parts returned to their respective origins in the sacrifice person Purusha. Basic to the Vedic sacrificial worldview, as noted above, is a synchronous construction of a world (the unmanifest Purusha-Prajapati) and of a self for the sacrificer. In ritual terminology the word for the body or self constructed in the center of the fire altar for *shrauta* performances is *atman*. This word became the key to a new vision of human destiny when it was declared to be ultimate reality, the unmanifest, *brahman*.

The *Chandogya*, an early Upanishad linked by tradition to a lost Brahmana of the *Samaveda*, is a good example of how the Upanishads could remain embedded in traditional sacrificial thought processes while inventing radical new expectations. It begins by exploring the mystical connection (*upanishad*) between the chant and the essence (*rasa*) of all cosmic entities, including the elements, speech, syllable, breath, mind, and so forth. It is of course the responsibility of the Samaveda chanter (*udgata*) to know these infinite identities and to involve himself with knowledge, faith, and insight into the inner workings of the *soma* sacrifice.

The *Chandogya Upanishad* never lets go of the significance of the chant (*saman*, *udgitha*) in the context of world-maintaining sacrifice. But quickly another agenda surfaces: study, meditation, concentration upon the infinite identities arrives at the point of ultimate breakthrough, that is, a recognition of the eternal, universal, absolute Self (*atman*) and its identity with *brahman*. The *atman-brahman* homology is the ultimate correspondence, beyond which no further search is possible.

It is revealing to note that in these discourses on the character of the *atman* the essential threefold and fivefold structure of the Self is a constant subject, involving a functional division of fires, breaths, and senses within one body, as well as in the processes of digestion, speech, and breathing. Abstraction is the language, the sacrificial terminology referring constantly to the offering of mystical substances. And in this fashion the sequential passage known as transmigration (*samsara*) comes under scrutiny. Transmigration according to *Chandogya* 5 is nothing other than a series of offerings into five successive cosmic fires, the fifth being woman, from whom the embryo (*garbha*) is born as the soul passes by ritual labor into yet another embodiment following the offering up of a previous one.

The link between the rebirth of a lifebody and ritual action (*karma*) is explained further by this same Upanishad. After death the soul ascends on one of two paths. The souls of those who perform rituals and good works go on the "path of the Fathers" to the world of the ancestors and then to the moon to become food (*soma*) for the gods. When the results of their previous actions (note that *karma* is now not limited to ritual action) can no longer maintain them in heaven they rain down in to the earth, grow as vegetation, and become food once again, this time for humans and animals. And again dependent upon the fruits of previous action, the eaten becomes like the eater, blessed or burdened with rank, from that of the Brahman, Kshatriya, or Vaishya down to rebirth as a Chandala (the lowest of human outcastes, beneath the Shudras), or a dog or a pig. By contrast the souls of those with knowledge—not of the rituals but of the imperishable *atman*—go by the "path of the gods" to *brahman* and immortality; they do not return, they have achieved *moksha*, release from the cycle of birth-death-rebirth. Knowledge of the *atman-brahman* identity wins over knowledge of the world-recycling ritual.

The sixth chapter of the *Chandogya*, reminiscent of the Purusha hymn in its division into sixteen parts, places all of this in proper perspective. The chapter concerns Svetaketu, who follows his father's advice and follows *brahmacharya*, the Vedic student's life, from age twelve to twenty-four. Having mastered the Vedic texts and rituals he is chagrined to discover—from the same father who encouraged him to learn the Vedas—that he is quite ignorant of what is supremely important, knowledge of the Self. And so his father instructs him in sixteen lessons about the highest truth. Each of the last nine lessons ends with a famous refrain, *tat tvam asi svetaketo iti* ("YOU are that, Svetaketu!", YOU are *brahman*, the absolute, the highest Self).

Like many reformations the Upanishadic one returns to religious roots (the Purusha hymn, basic sacrificial procedures, correspondences between the manifest and unmanifest realms). But also like many reformations a reshaping of basic religious expressions for a new era is in order. The static teaching of the Vedas and the mindless performance of ritals (Svetaketu's twelve-year education, useless from the perspective of salvation) are subordinated to the inner quest, mystical insight into transcendent selfhood, and an interior or meditational form of sacrifice.

The Upanishads also reintroduce the gods to center stage of Indian religious experiences. They have been there all the while, invited to the sacrifices and dismissed from them by the chants of the priests, but not since the powerful hymns of the *Rigveda* have they been so prominent in Vedic experience. The ritual work and godlike workers were always in the spotlight. A section of *Chandogya Upanishad* 3 describes the *atman* in strongly devotional language: the *atman* in the heart is *brahman*, and "on departing [this lifebody] I shall enter into him."

But it is the later verse Upanishads that introduce a theistic, even a sectarian note, moving from the Purusha-Prajapati and *atman-brahman* identities to embrace Ishvara, the Lord, as supremely worthy of meditation and praise. The *Shvetashvatara Upanishad* quotes extensively from the hymn of Purusha (*Rigveda* 10.90) and identifies him with Rudra, also called Shiva ("auspicious"). He is eternal, the one god without a second who lives in the hearts of all beings and brings cessation of birth to those who truly know him. The poetry of the *Katha Upanishad* also reveals this theistic trend. One who reins in with **yoga** his body, senses, and mind as a charioteer controls his horses and chariot will attain the highest abode of Vishnu.

Alongside the clarification of *samsara*, an expanded definition of *karma*, the interiorization of sacrifice, an emphasis on techniques of *yoga*, and the re-introduction of theism, the Upanishads were innovative in several other ways. They were now teachings with a more open transmission, primarily but not exclusively Brahman and masculine. Kshatriyas, women, others became "knowers" and teachers of the mystical connections because access to knowledge was no longer a birthright. Meditation, effort, striving, exertion—all of the experiences of Prajapati working toward creation or the renouncer working toward salvation—became hallmarks. References also were made to the careers of the student, householder, and mendicant-renunciant or forest hermit, later to be arranged as a program of life stages or *ashramas*. Finally, it might be said that the genre itself was an innovation, for post-Vedic "upanishads" continued to be composed over succeeding centuries until eventually more than a hundred were known.

Most of the significant developments in the religions of India in the classical or epic age, and the following medieval and modern periods, have partial or substantial bases in the Upanishads, from the all-encompassing themes of devotion (**bhakti**), to traditions of Tantra with esoteric attempts to establish divine androgyny, to the philosophical schools of Advaita Vedanta developed by Shankara, Ramanuja, and their successors.

■

CHAPTER III

Hinduism and History: The Epic Through Modern Periods

Ravana (the demon king who has abducted Sita, wife of Rama, and carried her off to his palace in Lanka): "O beautiful one! Wherever on your body I set my eyes, there they remain fixed and immovable. Accept me and enjoy all the pleasures of the world."

Sita: "How can I become your wife when I am the wife of another? Do not violate dharma. I belong to Rama as the Veda belongs to one who has reverently mastered it. Even now I hear the twang of Rama's bow. You cannot escape him."

Ravana: "Change your mind. Be my wife and come to my bed. If you refuse you will be sent to my kitchen and cooked for my meal. Beware!"

Valmiki's *Ramayana*[3]

For nearly a millennium and a half the Vedas were the dominant sound and authority of northern India. By the early centuries of the Common Era, however, two huge Sanskrit epics had begun to command the religious imagination and energy of Hinduism. Although eventually classified as **smriti**, tradition—and therefore subordinate to the Vedas in authority—these two verse dramas soon eclipsed all Vedic texts in popular religious life. To this day almost every Hindu knows the basic outline and scores of major and minor episodes in both the *Mahabharata* and the *Ramayana*. Frequently, this familiarity is doubled. Not only are portions of the Sanskrit epics known from local recitations, temple iconography, traveling performers, radio, film, and now television productions, but also from regional versions in the many spoken languages of India, popularized in the same versatile range of media.

One region—Tamil Nadu in South India—produced a classical civilization to rival that of the North and of Sanskrit. And one of its many assets was an epic tradition, displayed for example in the most famous of Tamil literary epics, the fifth-century *Cilappatikaram,* as well as later in the medieval period in Kampan's twelfth-century version of the *Ramayana,* and Villiputtur Alvar's *Mahabharata* composed about 1400 and completed by another poet in the eighteenth century.

Classical Indian Civilization

The lengthy period in which the Sanskrit epics were in the process of formation in North India ushers in the classical age not only of Hinduism but of Indian civilization at large. Epics were not the only extra-Vedic expression to emerge in the final centuries of the first millennium BCE. Legal, ethical, ritual, medical, philosophical, grammatical, astronomical, and many other interests were served textually, with classical Sanskrit the medium for an astonishing range of disciplines and schools. As noted previously, the various branches of Vedic tradition produced *sutra*s for both domestic and priestly ritual schedules. These were soon supplemented by law codes known as Dharma Sutras with instructions about proper conduct in all aspects of life. Few Dharma Sutras survived, but their subjects were later codified in verse in texts known as Shastras, and the Dharma Shastras remain today an established genre for Hindu religious life in general. The Laws of Manu, or Manava Dharma Shastra, cited in chapter one, is among the most significant.

More specialized, but also an outgrowth of the Vedic schools and their textual or ritual requirements, were the Vedangas, "limbs of the Veda." One concerned a combination of astronomy and astrology, a result of the obligation to match celestial and sacrificial precision and publish an exact ritual calendar. Another grew from a demand for textual precision, and grammar, etymology, lexicography, phonetics, and metrics were all initially born from this need for exactitude in the transmission of *shruti*.

In addition there were the beginnings of philosophical schools such as Mimamsa—adhering closely to analysis of Vedic ritual—and others such as Samkhya, Yoga, and Nyaya with agendas of speculation far removed from Vedic textual or ritual interests.

In this same period the unsystematized traditions of mantric healing known in the *Atharvaveda* gave precedence to new schools of medicine. Physicians grounded their practice on the theory that the human body functions with three humors in active correspondence with cosmic entities. The Sanskrit texts of Charaka and Sushruta, plus later works from the medieval period, are still today the basis of traditional medicine known as the Veda of long life, Ayurveda.

In other words, the building blocks of classical Indian civilization were laid in relatively short order in the late first millennium BCE and the early centuries CE. The Gupta dynasty, under four successive rulers from about 320 to 454, was able to unify politically most of the small kingdoms of North India and to influence both politically and culturally several regions of the South as well. At this time, in the fourth and fifth centuries CE, Indian culture reached its high point, a golden age of productivity in literature, philosophy, art, architecture, music, dance, drama, and—evident in all of these—religion.

By the middle centuries of the first millennium CE, after the compilation of both Sanskrit epics and with classical Indian civilization at its zenith, two important new types of Sanskrit texts emerged. One was the Puranas, collections of "old stories," that is, myths, folklore, temple legends, and details on everything from the creation of the world and the genealogies of gods and heroes to the significance of *dharma,* class and caste, asceticism, rituals, pilgrimages, and other acts of devotion to deities. Of course, the related concepts of *samsara, karma,* and *moksha* were never out of focus. Aside from their contents an important factor in the development of the Puranas was a regional one, as urban temples, festivals, pilgrimages, and localized mythologies, legends, and folklore gained prominence by the publicity of a Purana. Eventually a standard list of eighteen great Puranas surfaced, but the genre, once established, continued with hundreds of minor textual traditions.

There was another Sanskrit textual tradition that incorporated "old" material in a new form during the middle centuries of the first millennium CE. The Tantras, esoteric texts promoting liberation by radical beliefs and practices, were produced by Buddhist and Hindu schools alike. After the destruction of Buddhist monasteries in the medieval period Buddhist Tantrism survived as the "diamond vehicle," Vajrayana, in the Himalayas. Hindu Tantrism, on the other hand, became a significant element on the more provocative and experimental wing of Hindu tradition. A remarkable spiritual discipline evolved centering on mystical identification with masculine divine power, particularly the heroic form of the god Shiva, in order to unite with and be liberated by feminine cosmic energy (shakti). Various yogic techniques of long standing in South Asia were combined with erotic mysticism—partly traceable in the Upanishads, but mostly non-Aryan in origins. The emergence of goddesses into devotional prominence coincided with these practices, and eventually two paths were declared for Tantric devotees. One is the righthand, safe path of the conventional *yogin* or bhakta, the other the lefthand, dangerous and radical path of one who breaks the code of *dharma* in order to be liberated from all constraints. Typical of the latter is the practice of a ritual set of "five M's," community worship involving men and women employing five items that begin with the letter "M" in Sanskrit: eating meat, fish, and parched grains; drinking an alcoholic beverage; engaging in sexual intercourse as heroic Shiva and as Goddess or Shakti in order to attain a transcendent, genderless unity.

Some of the prominent themes of Yoga, the Puranas, and the Tantras will be pursued in chapter four. It was the Sanskrit epics that left the strongest mark on the period subsequent to the major Upanishads. The two together—the *Mahabharata* and the *Ramayana*—identify an age.

The Mahabharata

A popular tradition points to Vyasa, the "Arranger," as compiler of the larger of the two Sanskrit epics, the *Mahabharata* or Great Bharata. But the epic as it is known to scholars in eighteen long books and a total of nearly 100,000 verses was probably in a continuous state of composition and reformulation for many centuries between the fourth century BCE and the fourth century CE. Some scholars propose that key themes of the *Mahabharata,* including some with counterparts in other Indo-European epic traditions, may have been brought to India early in the first millennium BCE by a later Indo-Aryan-speaking culture, one substantially different from that of the earliest Vedic period.

Bharata is the name of an ancient hero. It is also an area of North India between the Himalaya and the Vindhya mountain ranges and the scene of a gripping drama, a land contested by two powerful sides of one family. One side includes the sons of Dhritarashtra; they are known as the Kauravas. Their cousins on the other side are known as the **Pandavas,** sons of Pandu, the younger brother of Dhritarashtra. While the Kauravas number a hundred heroes, with Duryodhana as their champion, the Pandavas count five brothers as principals: Yudhisthira, the eldest; **Arjuna,** the noblest warrior; Bhima, a rough-hewn guerrilla fighter; and the amiable twins Nakula and Sahadeva.

The opening book of the epic establishes a bad guys versus good guys plot, with the horde of Kauravas cast as demons and instigators of disorder. The Pandava heroes, on the other hand, are projections of specific functions of the foremost Vedic gods, and together they fight on the side of *dharma.* Arjuna, for example, was actually fathered by the great warrior god Indra, and the twins are the transposition into heroic form of the divine twins of Rigvedic mythology, the Ashvins. Like gods and demons, however, the heroes on both sides are not always predictable, and in true epic fashion they display the full range of human emotions and actions, not omitting valor and treachery.

In the city of Hastinapura the two sets of cousins are drawn into a game of chance. Yudhisthira, in a fit of gambling addiction, dices away his kingdom, his brothers, and even **Draupadi**, the common wife of all five Pandava heroes. They are forced into exile in the forest for thirteen years, after which Duryodhana reneges on his promise to return the Pandavas' portion of the kingdom. The middle books of the epic detail the great war that ensues, culminating in the slaughter of Duryodhana and most of his army, then a retaliatory night raid in which the carnage now embraces the children of the Pandavas and their troops. Only the five Pandava heroes survive among the lamentations of the women. Yudhisthira becomes universal emperor by the performance of the horse sacrifice (*ashvamedha*), and eventually the five heroes journey up into the Himalayas in an "ascent to heaven," the title of the final book.

The third episode of the sixth book is a Hindu classic known as the *Bhagavad Gita*. It serves not only as a condensation of themes in the epic itself, but also as a distillation of the Hindu worldview in the emergent classical age. The setting is a dramatic one of the moment before battle. **Krishna,** a counselor to the Pandavas, serving here as Arjuna's charioteer, instructs him about the eternal Self that cannot be killed, about the three paths to salvation—devotion, action, and knowledge (*bhakti, karma,* **jnana**)—and about the performance of one's own duty (*dharma*). In one powerful scene Arjuna asks Krishna to reveal himself as he really is, and Arjuna is able to experience, briefly, the awesome splendor of the transcendent god Vishnu.

The whole of the *Mahabharata* defies analysis. It has been aptly labeled a library rather than a text, since it includes a vast range of materials composed over a period of eight or more centuries. It contains even a version of the other epic, the *Ramayana*. And like epics in other cultures it is rich territory for scholarly interpretation. The great themes of Vedic mythology and ritual, some of them transparently Indo-European, have been transposed from the mythic to the epic sphere. The god Vishnu appears in the form of Krishna to assure the triumph of *dharma* and the defeat of chaos. The nature of deity—sometimes detached, sometimes immanent—is ambiguous, however, and the price of victory is heavy and includes, like sacrifice, death and destruction as a prelude to regeneration. Although renunciation and asceticism have their place, the *Bhagavad Gita* and the epic in general place an enduring stamp of approval on proper human activity in this world, including selfless devotion to God and selfless action in accord with *dharma*.

The Ramayana

The *Ramayana* shares a number of features with the *Mahabharata:* dynamic opposition of good and evil, exile in the forest, heroic combat, the victory of *dharma* over *adharma,* even a performance of the horse sacrifice near the close of the epic. And both achieved extended popularity with versions in regional languages in the medieval period. On the whole, however, they are substantially different. The *Ramayana,* only one-fourth the length of the *Mahabharata,* is tighter in focus as it unfolds its core narrative about the adventures of Rama and his wife **Sita.** Ascribed by tradition to the poet Valmiki, it is considered to be the first structured literary work in Sanskrit, crafted with metaphor, simile, and elaborate ornamentation that typify the poetic genre known as *kavya.*

The scene of this epic is well to the east of the Pandava-Kaurava kingdoms, in the city of Ayodhya. Rama, eldest son of King Dasharatha, wins the hand of the beautiful Sita by stringing the ponderous bow of the god Shiva. Court intrigue among the wives of Dasharatha forces the king's hand and, reluctantly, he satisfies a boon granted to his youngest wife and sends Rama and Sita into forest exile for fourteen years. After numerous adventures **Ravana,** a demon king of Lanka, falls in love with Sita, disguises himself as an ascetic, and contrives to carry her off to the South to his fortress in Lanka. A long campaign to retrieve Sita from the ten-headed Ravana ends in the siege and defeat of Lanka and the death of Ravana. In the war Rama and his brother **Lakshmana** have valu-

A Ramayana *panel sculpted on the wall of a Hindu temple compound about 900* CE *on the island of Java in Indonesia. An army of monkeys hurls boulders into a monster-filled sea, building a causeway to rescue Sita from Lanka.*

able assistance from Sugriva, the monkey king, and **Hanuman,** his champion. Rama is crowned king in Ayodhya with Sita restored to his side.

The citation at the head of this segment sets the tone of this romantic drama: Ravana lusts after his captive princess, but the damsel in distress resists and furthermore shames him by preaching about *dharma* and the Vedas. Sita retains her virtue until the rescue. However, the seventh and final book, considered by most scholars to be a later addition, rewrites the ending. The people of Ayodhya do not believe that Sita resisted the ten-headed demon. Rama accedes to their protests and reluctantly banishes his queen. A distraught Sita beseeches the earth goddess to validate her innocence (her name, sita, is the plowed "furrow," and she was born from the earth mother). The earth swallows her forever.

The characters are ideal types, Rama being the heroic, vigorous, princely figure, Sita the beautiful, virtuous, loyal wife. Their divinity is established only in the first and last books. It is in the regional versions that the transformation of hero to god, heroine to goddess is complete. In the vernacular epics Rama is an incarnation of Vishnu, Sita an incarnation of Vishnu's consort **Lakshmi.** Hanuman, the monkey ally, plays another ideal role, that of supreme devotee, and his enormous strength and devotion are always in the service of Rama. By extension he too became the center of human devotional attention and has his own *bhakta*s.

The medieval epics based on the Sanskrit or Valmiki *Ramayana* include the *Iramavataram,* composed in the twelfth century in Tamil by Kamban; the *Ramacaritmanas,* composed in Hindi by Tulsi Das; the Telugu *Ranganatha Ramayana:* and the Krittivas *Ramayana* in Bengali. Episodes from the *Ramayana* (and *Mahabharata*) also were the material of the sacred shadow puppet dramas (*wayang kulit*) of Javanese tradition.

Vishnu, Shiva, and the Goddess

More than a millennium separates the period of the major Upanishads and the medieval period of Indian civilization. During these many centuries the two epics were composed, shaped, and reshaped, gradually incorporating a synthesis of Hindu tradition.

The classical civilizations based on Sanskrit in the north and Tamil in the deep south reached their full productivity; Puranas and Tantras developed as new genres alongside the older Dharma Shastra and epic texts. It was in this period that Hinduism achieved its classical, that is to say, definitive guise.

With the re-emergence of theism in the late centuries BCE came the opportunity for *bhakti,* the devotional tradition, to achieve status not only as one among several options for religious expression, but as the dominant path toward salvation. Two figures emerge, Vishnu and Shiva, each with a full range of expressions that continue essential elements of myths, rites, and symbols of the past—Vedic and non-Vedic—and each in position to move on this new tide of devotional energy across the subcontinent. They are joined by an array of local, regional, and pan-Indian goddesses who achieve equal status and in some cases (village goddesses, Tantric circles) higher prominence in popular affection.

The two Sanskrit epics include key figures who become in the course of the epic age the two most prominent **avataras** "descents" or incarnations of the great deity Vishnu. Krishna of the *Bhagavad Gita* and Rama of the *Ramayana* indicate the priority of these two *avataras*. Eventually lists of ten or more *avataras* appear, and Vishnu becomes almost a pantheon in his own right. In the process of assembling this system of *avataras* several regional deities were incorporated. Active sects in the last centuries BCE included the Bhagavatas, worshipers of Bhagavan, the Lord (Vishnu), originating in the area of Mathura in North India. Another that appears eventually to have merged with the Bhagavatas was the Pancharatras, a sect centering on Narayana. The twelfth book of the *Mahabharata* contains a section extolling Narayana-Vishnu. Still another early movement seems to have focused on a clan deity, Vasudeva, later identified with Krishna. One of the principal doctrines to emerge in these centuries was that of *vyuha*s or emanations of Vishnu, five manifestations of God that correspond to the five regions of the macrocosmos and the five aspects of the human microcosmos. In the Tamil south between the seventh and tenth centuries CE there developed a tradition of Vishnu *bhakta*s known as the Alvars. Eventually twelve in number, these poet-saints, mostly non-Brahmans, deepened the basis of devotional Hinduism into all strata of Hindu society.

The twelve Alvars complemented a traditional medieval list of sixty-two or sixty-three poet-saints expressing devotion to Shiva in their Tamil verses composed between the sixth and ninth centuries. Perhaps the earliest of these Nayanmars, as they are known collectively, was a woman devotee of Shiva, Karaikkal Ammaiyar. Earlier than the Nayanmars of the south, however, were the Pashupatas, worshipers of Pashupati, Lord of Creatures, identified with Shiva. These communities, mentioned in the *Mahabharata,* developed distinctive ritual patterns and ascetic traditions until the medieval period. By the medieval period numerous Shaiva sects were active in both north and south, including Shaiva Siddhanta in Tamil Nadu, the Virashaivas or Lingayats throughout the Deccan, and Kashmiri Shaivism in the far northwest.

Already mentioned are the epic heroines Draupadi of the *Mahabharata* and Sita of the *Ramayana.* Both may be seen in the long-term development of devotional tradition as incarnations of Vishnu's consort Lakshmi or Shri, although Sita demonstrates possibly much older characteristics as an earth or agrarian goddess. It is in the *Markandeya Purana,* however, that the Hindu goddesses are finally recognized and synthesized in all their power. The Devi Mahatmya section, probably sixth century CE, celebrates **Durga** as the invincible slayer of the buffalo-headed demon **Mahisha,** who has threatened the world. Vishnu, Shiva, all the other gods are powerless before him, but the inexhaustible interior strength of the goddess prevails, and Durga mounted on her lion is victorious.

The mythologies and rituals of Krishna, Rama, **Narasimha,** and other *avatara*s of Vishnu; of Nataraja, Bhairava, and other forms of Shiva; and of Durga, **Kali, Parvati,** and other manifestations of the Goddess, will be further explored in chapter four.

Medieval South Asia

> The Chandogya Upanishad can describe the various components of the sacrifice of breath only by way of such imaginary correspondences as "the chest is the sacrificial area, the hairs are the sacrificial grass, the heart is the cooking fire, the mind is the defensive fire, the mouth is the offering fire."
>
> Shankara, Commentary on the *Brahma Sutra* of Badarayana

Feet, navel, hands,
 chest, eyes, and lips
red-rayed jewels
 set in a blue glow,
and golden silks round his waist,
my lord is all blaze and dazzle:
I do not know how to reach him.
Nammalvar, Tamil poet[4]

In this overview of history and Hinduism, *medieval* ("middle age") refers to a thousand-year period midway between the classical age in which the Sanskrit epics were formed and the modern age shaped by contact with the Western world. The time frame for this epoch is roughly 750 CE to 1750 CE.

Two great synthesizing minds stand out during the early medieval period. Shankara opens this age and Ramanuja appears about three centuries later. Both were Brahmans born in South India, both were scholars and writers of influential Sanskrit commentaries on the classic Sanskrit texts, and both were strong-willed institution builders responsible for much in the patterns of Hindu thought and practice today.

And two significant events are prominent in the later centuries of the medieval period. Islam made its presence known in the subcontinent only gradually between the seventh and twelfth centuries, then more impressively with the Delhi sultanate in the thirteenth century. Almost the entire region was unified politically by 1600 after the conquests of Akbar, third and greatest of the Mughal emperors to rule India. Although the Mughal empire began to unravel in the eighteenth century, from Akbar's reign until the present day Islam has been an effective religious and cultural force in many areas of the subcontinent; it is the state religion in both Pakistan and Bangladesh. The Hindu-Muslim encounter is one of the definitive events of medieval South Asia.

The other late medieval phenomenon was a remarkable new surge of devotional theism throughout India, together with the wider appearance of vernacular languages as voices of revitalized Hindu faith. *Bhakti,* openly declared in the Sanskrit *Bhagavad Gita* and the Tamil poems from devotees of Vishnu and Shiva, established itself permanently in each of the multiple tongues of India.

Shankara and Advaita Vedanta

Reflection on the past is appropriate as a person begins middle age; and Shankara, more than anyone, was the reflective mind of Indian civilization as it approached its own middle years. A review and assessment of classical thought is precisely what he accomplished for medieval India.

Although Shankara is recognized as one of the two most creative Hindu thinkers subsequent to the period of the Upanishads, his life is so buried under saintly legends that nothing can be said about him without the preface "according to one tradition." Not even the century in which he lived is certain, but the eighth is most probable, and Kerala is generally accepted as his birthplace. He is said to have taken vows of *samnyasa* already as a child and then to have traveled throughout India, first as student and later as teacher and founder of monastic centers (**mathas**). If the tradition that he lived for only thirty-two years is correct, then his genius flowered early and splendidly. In an effort almost mythic in scope, he is said to have established monasteries in each of the four corners of India: Badrinath, source of the Ganges in the Himalayan north; Puri, on the Bay of Bengal in the east: Sringeri and possibly also Kanchi in the Tamil south; and Dvaraka on the west coast. And tradition accords more than three hundred Sanskrit works to him, making Shankara a close rival to the legendary Vyasa as best-selling author—if only in honor and respect.

The most influential works that are authentically Shankara's were his commentaries on the *Brahma* (or *Vedanta*) *Sutras* of Badarayana and on certain major Upanishads. Since the *Brahma Sutras* (possibly a first century BCE work) are themselves terse commentaries on the major Upanishads, it is those works—about eight centuries old in Shankara's day—that command attention. Some of the later Upanishads used the term **vedanta,** "end of the Veda," with reference to their doctrines as a distillation of Vedic knowledge. This term became the name of a leading philosophical tradition among the six systems of Indian thought known as **darshanas**, or points of view. It was Shankara who shaped Vedanta, and the nondualistic or Advaita Vedanta tradition in particular.

By focusing on speculations in the Upanishads as scriptural authority (*shruti*) and linking those speculations to selected texts in tradition (*smriti*), Shankara was able to develop a coherent "point of view." It included the following observations. The Upanishads (and therefore the eternal Vedas) reveal a paramount instruction: only *brahman* is real. Since *brahman* is without duality (**advaita**), no distinctions are real. And *brahman,* the true Self, is not subject to *samsara.* A self caught in *samsara* makes distinctions, sees multiplicity, takes qualities for real because it is bound by ignorance (**avidya**) and illusion (**maya**). Enlightenment or liberation (*moksha*) of the self from *samsara* occurs through replacement of the wrong knowledge (*avidya*) with knowledge of the highest *brahman.* The object on the ground that was thought to be a snake turns out, on closer inspection, to be a rope. Likewise, said Shankara, where the self is concerned, the acquisition of true knowledge supplants ignorance and *samsara,* and the sole reality of *atman-brahman* as Self is recognized.

As an illustration of Shankara's scholarship and of the complicated interaction of textual and scholastic traditions in his day, consider the passage cited above. It is from the third lesson of his lengthy commentary on the work of Badarayana written perhaps seven or eight centuries earlier. Shankara's (and Badarayana's) concern is a passage in the *Chandogya Upanishad* (5.19.2) composed perhaps six centuries or so before Badarayana. Note that the subject is sacrifice, the central doctrine of the Vedas. But the attention of the Upanishad, Badarayana, and Shankara is not on the actual performance itself in all of its details. For that we should consult the Samhitas and Brahmanas, which Shankara refers to as the ritual (*karma*) portion of *shruti,* as distinct from the knowledge (*jnana*) portion of *shruti,* the Aranyakas and Upanishads. Nor is the attention of the *Chandogya Upanishad,* the Sutras, and Sankara's commentary on the mythic power of the cosmic person (Purusha) whose members and organs have become—in a set of correspondences as old as Proto–Indo-European tradition—world parts, including the sacrificial fires. Instead the focus is a symbolic sacrifice, an interior offering of breath within the absolute Self (*atman*), the world soul that is independent of any need of human offerings or acts of any sort whatever.

Shankara's position is even further removed from the condensed symbols of sacrifice in the Upanishad. He reviews the ancient set of sacrificial members not out of belief, but only to demonstrate their unreality; they are effective only by "imaginary correspondences," the result of *maya,* illusion. The highest *brahman* is devoid of qualities (chest, hair, heart, mind, mouth, and so forth), and Shankara is convinced that both *shruti* and *smriti* are agreed upon this fundamental truth. Quite simply put, the Vedic sacrificers appreciated, even revered the correspondences between the creative unmanifest and the created world, including human bodily parts in particular. Shankara dismissed these correspondences as a mistaken point of view.

For a parallel to this gradual theological march away from the graphic realities of blood sacrifice and a parallel also to this telescoping series of scriptural discourses and commentaries (Samhitas, Brahmanas, Upanishads, Sutras, Shankara's Advaita Vedanta), consider biblical tradition. There is considerable distance between animal sacrifice described in the Torah of ancient Israel, the symbolic interpretation of sacrifice in postexilic Judaism, its further extension in early Christianity in the letters of Paul, and finally the theology of Thomas Aquinas commenting on scripture and the Greek and Latin church fathers. This lineage moves from ancient Hebrew to Hellenistic Greek to medieval Latin, whereas Shankara's Sanskrit is not far removed from Vedic Sanskrit. In terms of religious expression, however, the gradual abstraction of sacrifice is not dissimilar, there are parallel strategies to align scripture and subsequent "tradition," and the textual time span is more than two millennia in both situations.

Ramanuja and Developing Bhakti

The other giant of the early medieval period was also a South Indian Brahman, learned traveler, teacher, and administrator. Educated in the Vedanta traditions at Kanchi, Ramanuja became a much-sought-after teacher in Tamil Nadu, probably in the early twelfth century. Like Shankara he was well versed in Vedic texts, and eventually he wrote commentaries, again like Shankara, on the major Upanishads and the *Brahma Sutras,* as well as a separate one on the *Bhagavad Gita.* His intense devotion to Vishnu, however, led him on a path that was different both intellectually and spiritually from that of his eighth-century predecessor.

Ramanuja was initiated into the Shri Vaishnava movement, a sect that looked for authority not only to the Vedas but also to the devotional songs of the Tamil Alvars. The Alvars were twelve poet-saints of the popular southern *bhakti* tradition. Perhaps the most famous of them was Nammalvar, whose verse in praise of Lord Vishnu is cited above (after the quote from Shankara). Written only a century before Ramanuja's time, this verse celebrates precisely the qualities of God discounted as unreal by Shankara's nondualism. Nammalvar's god is "all blaze and dazzle" and has a chest, eyes, and mouth like his devotee, or the *yogi* in concentration, or the meditating sacrificer who encompasses the world in his inner offering of breath, or the divine Purusha who becomes this world in sacrifice. Without performing sacrifices Nammalvar is doing what the Vedic sacrificers did, revering correspondences. But even with all of these divine/human mediations the poet still laments "I do not know how to reach him."

Ramanuja's Vedic upbringing and training in Vedanta were tempered by exactly this kind of popular theism. The result was his intellectual contribution to a school of "qualified" nondualism, Vishishtadvaita Vedanta. The point of departure for this tradition is *brahman* as Brahman, that is, as God, Ishvara, the Lord, a Supreme Being with attributes and personality. Whereas Shankara maintained *brahman* as impersonal and without qualities (*nirguna*), Ramanuja and his school of Vedanta insisted upon *brahman* as personal and with qualities (*saguna*). *Brahman* is truth, knowledge, infinity. And yet Ramanuja, too, upheld the oneness, the nonduality of *brahman*.

Two additional features of Ramanuja's theology signaled his departure from the position established by Shankara. First, whereas Shankara maintained that both a lower knowledge (of rituals) and a higher knowledge (of *brahman*) were revealed in the Upanishads, Ramanuja understood the instruction of the Upanishads to be uniform and undivided. The world in which rituals are performed is real, and therefore a source of knowledge and truth; positive results from worship and devotion are to be recognized in this world. Second, Shankara taught that the revelation of the Upanishads concerning the identity of *atman-brahman* meant the merger of the individual soul into the absolute soul. Since distinctions prevail only in *samsara* and are due to illusion and ignorance, *moksha* reveals the supreme truth: there is no individual self. Ramanuja, on the other hand, taught that the individual self is a distinct personality, eternal even after liberation.

Like Shankara before him Ramanuja founded *mathas* in various locations. Tradition credits him with establishing seventy-four Vaishnava centers in a lifetime of 120 years. Equally important was his effort in the reform of temple ritual. As a temple priest at Kanchi, and later as head priest of the huge staff of the Ranganatha temple at Srirangam, he had ample opportunity to insert his interpretations of *shruti* and *smriti* into the daily liturgies. Many of his reforms are both visible and audible today in the great Vaishnava temples of the south.

In sum, Ramanuja effected a compromise that became the Hindu mainstream. He reconciled the Sanskrit textual tradition of the Brahmans, including both the Vedas and the post-Vedic Sutras and epics (the *Bhagavad Gita* in particular) with the Tamil textual

Part of a swiftly moving crowd of nearly one million pilgrims of all castes on the way to the temple of the god Vithoba in Pandharpur in western India. They walk barefoot for fifteen days, following the route of medieval saints and singing their devotional songs.

tradition of popular non-Brahman poet-saints. Ramanuja provided authoritative philosophical and liturgical voices for the devotional tradition that he himself—through personal experience in the worship of Vishnu and Lakshmi—valued as deeply as the Upanishadic-Vedantic tradition of nonduality. In this respect his efforts resembled those of al-Ghazzali, the great Muslim teacher and writer who provided—also from intense personal experience—theological credentials for the popular devotional and mystical traditions of Sufism in twelfth-century Baghdad. Interestingly enough, Ramanuja and al-Ghazzali—separated by religion, culture, and geography—were contemporaries, and their respective reforms would meet one another in India only a few generations later.

Early in the fourteenth century Ramanuja's school of Vedanta became divided over issues of divine grace and human action. Both were agreed upon *bhakti* as the path of release. Their differences, however, were popularized in the Tamil country by reference to two animal mothers saving their young in crises. When a kitten is in danger the mother cat springs to it, picks it up by the scruff of the neck, and carries it to safety. A baby monkey in danger jumps onto the back of the mother, clasps her neck, and is carried to safety. The "cat's way," as it came to be known, is the way of divine salvation by God's grace alone. Like the kitten dangling in the air, an individual soul can do nothing to earn release from *samsara* and must therefore surrender and become absolutely dependent. The "monkey's way," by contrast, teaches cooperative effort alongside grace; like the baby monkey's act of holding on, human action as well as God's grace is essential, and initiative does count as merit toward eventual release.

Islam and Hinduism

All four of the great religions that emerged in West Asia—Zoroastrianism, Judaism, Christianity, and Islam—were established in South Asia during the first millennium CE. Whereas Jews and the Parsis (Zoroastrians) remained tiny regional minorities on the west coast of India, Christians and Muslims both became multiform traditions that gradually spread throughout South Asia. Of the four, however, only Islam became a state religion, and this occurred in the Mughal empire in the late medieval period.

Already within a century of the death of the Prophet Muhammad in 632, Arabs raided outlying settlements in the northwest of India. From the eighth to the fifteenth centuries successive waves of ethnic Muslims entered the subcontinent—Arabs, Turks, Afghans, Persians, Mongols. Raiders came to loot the palaces, treasuries, and temples, but it was the settled merchants and other colonists who slowly spread the new religion. A confessional faith, Islam presented itself as the mirror opposite of Hinduism: a strict monotheism with a sacred book, the word of Allah in an Arabic Qur'an, revealed through his messenger, the Prophet Muhammad; a single community with a single law and the notion of an abode of Islam (*dar al-Islam*) in which religion and polity are one; a doctrine of the unity of God that has no place for iconography, let alone myths, symbols, and rituals celebrating the dynamic multiplicity of the divine. This vigorous new faith was presented lucidly and aggressively.

By the thirteenth century political control came into the hands of the Muslims of the Delhi sultanate. With Arabic the language of religion, and Persian the language of government, literature, and the arts, the Sanskrit base and Brahman hegemony of North Indian civilization were seriously challenged. By the sixteenth century Islam stretched from Europe to China and Indonesia and surpassed Buddhism as the most extensive world religion in Asia. The Mughal dynasty in South Asia surfaced as the easternmost of three great empires alongside the Ottomans in southeastern Europe, Anatolia, North Africa, and West Asia, and the Safavids in Iran and Afghanistan. By 1600 the military genius of Akbar, third Mughal emperor, brought political unification to the subcontinent, and by 1700 that control was virtually total. Aurangzeb, the last great Mughal, was a ruler by confrontation as far as non-Muslims were concerned. Hindus were forced to pay the poll tax for the unbelievers; destruction of Hindu *mathas*, temples, pilgrimage sites, and iconography was at its height. But by 1800 the Mughal empire had all but collapsed, and with it the dream of a *dar al-Islam*. (Only after independence from the British in 1947 did the partition of India create the modern Islamic state of Pakistan; eventually, East Pakistan became Bangladesh, also an Islamic state.)

The net result of this event of Islam that occupied the entire medieval period is informative. Hindus who did not convert were liable to the more or less restrictive poll tax known as *jizya,* but by and large they went on as before. As a tradition, Hinduism was apparently not impressed by any of the six statements of belief or the five practices, those straightforward articles of faith that make Sunni Islam—of all world religions—one of the most lucid and declarative. On the other hand, Islam found itself drawn ineluctably into a process of South Asianization, a series of minor modifications already evident by the end of the medieval period. Such modifications—significant only in aggregate, and variable by region—still continue today in the nation of India, where Islam is a minority faith. They include observance of castelike hierarchies and restrictions, complete with a continuum running between those peoples regarded as pure or clean and those regarded as polluted or unclean; recognition of *guru*like preceptors with great spiritual powers and of *yogi*like or *sadhi*like mendicants with special skills or roles; particular expressions in prayers and devotions; tantra or *yoga*like techniques of meditation; life-cycle rituals similar to Hindu *samskaras*; participation in local or pan-Indian pilgrimages and festivals; and above all, worship at the tombs of saints and reliance upon the powers of saints for personal needs such as childbirth, healing, release from demons, and so forth. Despite the presence of one or several of these special features of South Asian Islam, the average Muslim continued to subscribe to most of the requisite articles of belief and practice in Sunni custom.

It was the Sufi mystics in several orders established in India between the thirteenth and sixteenth centuries whose spiritual quests and recognition of divine immanence were most in tune with the experimental, eclectic, and individualist modes of Hinduism. Among the half dozen major orders were the Chishti brought from Afghanistan, the Suhrawardi from the area of Baghdad, and later the Shattari and Naqshbandi. It was not only spiritual guidance proved by the *pir* or *shaykh* and initiation onto the path and into the order that found a match in Hindu traditions of *guru,* disciple, path, and order. There were also discussions of the proper recipe of divine grace and guided human action, the reality or unreality of the world and of the self, and the union with God as partial or complete. All these discussions were similar to debates among followers of various schools of Vedanta, Yoga, and Samkhya. And Sufis spoke of a choice between spiritual modes, a hazardous and a safe mode, for example, parallel to traditions of Tantric Yoga with its left- and righthand paths. Certain techniques on the path such as breath-control and devotional, even ecstatic recitation of the divine names found a ready reception. And just as Sufi teachers were effective in vernaculars elsewhere, so also in rural South Asia. Urdu, Bengali, Telugu, Marathi, and other regional languages of the late medieval period became the medium of expression to those without knowledge of the scriptural language, Arabic, or the official language, Persian.

One Chishti holy man so impressed the Mughal emperor Akbar that he moved his capital into a city newly constructed near the saint's remote residence. Fascinated with the diversity of active religions, Akbar built there a House of Worship in which debates were held. Invited were not only Sufis from the Chishti and other mystic orders, as well as Shi'a and Sunni Muslims, but also Vaishnava, Shaiva, Jaina, Jesuit, and Parsi authorities. Akbar later instituted a reconciling "religion of God" *(din-i ilahi)* in his court. Although short lived, it was one more sign of the remarkable religious pluralism of the late medieval period in which Islam, intent on domination, was reluctantly caught in a struggle for self-definition and an eventual compromise position as an influential minority faith.

Late Medieval *Bhakti*

Already mentioned were the impact of the *Bhagavad Gita* segment of the Sanskrit *Mahabharata*— in which *bhakti* is taught by Krishna-Vishnu as one of the three paths to release—and the devotional hymns of the Tamil poet-saints in praise of both Vishnu and Shiva. By the time the first southern expressions of *bhakti* emerged in the sixth and seventh centuries, the Sanskrit Puranas were well established as a genre of mythology, folklore, and regional tradition. Collections known as Puranas continued to form throughout the medieval period until eventually there were eighteen Sanskrit texts rivaling the epics for prominence. Some were Vaishnava, some Shaiva, some a mixture, and all found space for traditions of the regional and pan-Indian goddesses.

From the thirteenth to the seventeenth centuries great poet-saints to match the Alvars and Nayanmars of the south achieved fame in the west and north of India. Jnaneshvar (also known as Jnandev) brought Krishna-*bhakti* into regional prominence in the late thirteenth century with his popular treatise on the *Bhagavad Gita,* the *Jnaneshvari,* written in Marathi, the language of Maharashtra in western India. In the following centuries Namdev, Eknath, and Tukaram all composed their songs in Marathi in praise of great deities, temples, and pilgrimage traditions. Tukaram, a Shudra by birth, became the most celebrated of the western poet-saints.

In North India the prominent Hindi devotional poets included Tulsidas (author of the Hindi Ramayana mentioned earlier); Surdas, devotee of Lord Krishna and a poet-singer who, according to tradition, was blind; Mirabai, a Rajput princess and another devotee of Krishna who sang as a renunciant itinerant of her marriage to the dark Lord; and Raidas, a Chamar (Untouchable leather-worker) poet. The religious pluralism of late-medieval North India allowed for syncretic devotional traditions. Although born into a Muslim weaver family, the late-fifteenth century saint Kabir often referred to God as Ram (Rama); his iconoclastic verses were always quick, however, to reject any divine qualities, or any faith in images, rituals, or scriptures as means to salvation. Guru Nanak, credited with establishing the Sikh tradition in the late fifteenth century, and Dadu, founder of the Dadu Panth in the late sixteenth century, were two additional North Indians whose *bhakti* generated innovative followings.

In Bengal in the northeast, where Jayadeva composed in Sanskrit his famous love-song of Radha and Krishna known as the *Gita Govinda,* there were also great poet-saints composing in their native language, Bengali. Chandidas is the signature of many popular Bengali poems of the late medieval period, and Vidyapati, who wrote in the Maithili vernacular, was equally well loved in the late fourteenth and early fifteenth centuries. Mention should also be made of the sixteenth-century mystic and saint Chaitanya whose inspired devotion to Krishna was a stimulus to Vaishnava traditions throughout northeastern India. Although these centuries witnessed the decline of Buddhism, in Bengal the Tantric traditions in Buddhism as well as Hinduism continued to flourish, and the erotic mysticism of many Vaishnava and Shaiva devotional poems reflects a Tantric presence. Ramprasad Sen was an eighteenth-century Bengali poet celebrating the divine essence as *shakti,* feminine energy.

In sum these many poet-saints were key regional figures in the late medieval period. Instrumental sometimes in establishing regional variants of selected Sanskrit or Tamil classical traditions, they were even more effective in the spread of new institutions of followers who perpetuated their passionate celebration of the immanence of deity, the community of the faithful, and the ease of the divine-human encounter through music and song instead of priestly rituals, remote texts, and divisive laws. They also stimulated the growth of vernacular literatures in each major language region of the subcontinent.

Modern South Asia

> This ashram has been created . . . not for the renunciation of the world but as a center and field of practice for the evolution of another kind and form of life.
>
> *Aurobindo* (1872–1950)[5]

In the ancient period the demise of the Indus civilization was closely followed by the expansion of energetic new immigrants to the subcontinent—the Vedic pastoralists. Likewise, a five-century-old Muslim hegemony in South Asia gave way to vigorous new immigrants—the European colonial powers of the eighteenth century. The Portuguese, beginning with the navigator Vasco da Gama who opened the sea trade routes from East Africa in 1498, Dutch, French, Danes, and Germans all established colonies along the coasts of the peninsula. But it was the British with the East India Company who proved most capable in appropriating and consolidating territory. By the late eighteenth century, only a generation after the collapse of the Mughals, the British Raj was the new empire for the shaping of India over the next period of nearly two hundred years. The post–World War II era of dismantling colonial systems in Asia and Africa included India, and on Independence day, January 26, 1947, a new constitutional government succeeded England's rule.

The British Raj—a substantial period of modern political history although brief in South Asia's long memory—was an era of changes as rapid as they were radical. One shift was to a new language that remains to this day the language of commerce, government and the civil service, higher education, and large segments of the media, cultural institutions, and the arts (although an estimate is that only 2% of the total populace of India today speaks English). The Raj also introduced new social, political, and economic institutions. Eventually these would transform the many self-sufficient regional Hindu and Muslim kingdoms into clusters of viable economic areas connected physically by road, rail, and sea and linked ideologically by a common world language and a dynamic technology from the European industrial revolution. Great cities such as Bombay, Calcutta, and Madras arose from humble origins, and others like Delhi and Hyderabad were transformed by the urban style of the new rulers. Transformations in rural India and the bulk of the Hindu, Muslim, and tribal population were slower and less visible, but there too the effects of Western education, social reform, law, medicine, religion, literature, and the printing press were gradually evident. With the creation of an English-speaking, British-educated, often Christian-influenced elite, the stage was set for the appearance of several charismatic personalities in the nineteenth century.

Reformers and Traditionalists

Two imposing personalities stand out in the middle decades of the nineteenth century, each the founder of a society (*samaj*) concerned with redesigning Hinduism for a new age, each convinced that "the Vedas" were the proper basis for a renascent faith, each with an eye toward a pan-Indian reformation. But their experiences and agendas were substantially different. Ram Mohan Roy (1772–1833)—a Bengali Brahman intellectual who founded the Brahmo Samaj (Society) in 1828—traveled in England, was influenced early in life by the faith of Islam and by Christian missionaries, and thought of the Hindu tradition as unnecessarily burdened by image worship, polytheistic myths, vulgar festivals, knotty regulations of caste behavior, and limiting doctrines such as *samsara*.

In other words, all the things in Hinduism that puzzled Western observers began to appear to Ram Mohan Roy as extraneous to the real Hindu faith. He proposed the Upanishads, which he had already translated from Sanskrit into both English and Bengali, as the essence of the Vedas, and a rationalist, humanist basis for renovation. The society's meetings were in fact recognizable Protestant services with sermons based on Upanishads as scripture, hymn singing, and prayers addressed to the one supreme God revealed in the Upanishads. Debendranath Tagore (1817–1905), father of the Nobel prize–winning poet Rabindranath Tagore, and Keshab Chandra Sen (1838–1884) were later overseers of the society and one of its offshoots. The society's narrow regional base in Bengal and its elitist membership of upper-caste intellectuals rendered the movement ineffective in terms of its immodest goal of overturning some twenty-five centuries of the Hindu worldview.

A Gujarati Brahman named Dayananda Sarasvati (1824–1883) also preached a back-to-the-Vedas movement, but for him it was not the Upanishads but the *mantra*s of the *Rigveda* that held the key to Hindu reform. His interpretation of the *mantra*s was entirely idiosyncratic, for he found in them one supreme God only, as well as the doctrines of *karma* and *samsara*. Equally inventive was his notion of what was not in the *mantra*s, and that included any connection with the performance of sacrifices. The Arya Samaj that Dayananda founded in 1875 was for decades centered in another regional base, the Punjab, until it spread gradually through the Hindi-speaking north and became more successful than the Brahmo Samaj not only in geographical breadth but also in outreach to the several *varna*s as well. This new society became notorious, in fact, for investing untouchables with the sacred thread. Like the Brahmo Samaj, however, the Arya Samaj splintered into ineffectiveness over complicated issues of social reform and militant politics.

Quite different from these two reformers—each with an ideology intentionally undermining Puranic Hinduism in favor of a universal theism—were three other vigorous personalities—Ramakrishna, Vivekananda, and Aurobindo, founders of another pair of institutions still active in modern Hinduism in India and the West. Ramakrishna (1836–1886) was a Bengali Brahman temple priest and devotional mystic whose spiritual trek through

Yoga, Tantrism, Vedanta, Vaishnava theism, Christianity, and Islam never took him far from the feminine power (*shakti*) he worshiped as the goddess Kali. His principal disciple was Vivekananda (1863–1902), founder of the Ramakrishna Mission and order of swamis who today are more in accord with the philosophy of Advaita Vedanta than of Ramakrishna's eclectic mysticism. An event that every Indian child assimilates with pride in school is the 1893 assembly of the World Parliament of Religions in Chicago where Vivekananda "astounded the West" by his discourses on Hinduism, then went on to establish the Vedanta societies of New York, San Francisco, and other cities. The Ramakrishna Mission is still an influential force in towns and cities throughout India, with a significant charitable and educational outreach in medical clinics, pharmacies, publishing houses, and forums in their *matha*s for religious discourse. The compelling combination of Ramakrishna the visionary-saint and Vivekananda the missionary-orator accomplished more for the Hindu self-image in the community of world religions than any other movement until Gandhi.

Aurobindo (1872–1950) was another visionary of self-realization and interior harmony, well traveled and educated, versed in the full range of Vedic and Sanskrit classics and, like Ramakrishna, experienced in Tantric Yoga and imbued with reliance on the divine *shakti*. His three-volume *The Life Divine* became a modern classic with its optimistic program of progression from primal matter to perfect being, consciousness, and bliss. He lived in the French colony of Pondicherry in South India for most of his adult life; his place of residence grew into an ashram for his disciples and eventually into an international center for spiritual transformation. Subsequent to his death the ashram and its acolyte institutions were led by Aurobindo's companion of thirty years, Mme Mir Richard, a French woman known to devotees as the Mother.

These modern voices—Ram Mohan Roy, Dayananda Sarasvati, Ramakrishna, Vivekananda, Aurobindo—as well as many others like them might be described as reforming traditionalists or traditional reformers. Many were Bengalis; most were educated in British academies and spoke and wrote in English. Each maintained his personal perspective about what is enduring in Hinduism and what components should be promoted or eliminated in the ongoing experience and expression of the faith. All of them spoke of "self-realization," and in that sense they identified common ground in both the Upanishads and the traditions of Yoga. Each had a sphere of influence in the shaping of contemporary Indian thought and yet, so remote and sheltered is life in the world of village India that few of their names and fewer of their ideas evoked much response in their day, and villagers of the next century may forget them altogether.

One name, face, and figure of twentieth-century India, however, is known to all, as indeed he is instantly recognized, as few humans are, throughout the world. Mohandas K. Gandhi (1869–1948), the Mahatma or "Great Soul," a lawyer from a Vaishya family in western India, became one of the architects of Indian independence, a champion of *svaraj* (self-rule) through *satyagraha* (a grasping of the truth), of nonviolent resistance to evil and oppression. The *Bhagavad Gita* and its doctrine of detached action became his spiritual guide, and a life of simple self-sufficiency and chastity (*brahmacharya*) his well-publicized life-style. But even the powerful personality of Gandhi with his demonstrative *dharma* could not prevent the Hindu-Muslim mutual slaughter that accompanied independence and the 1947 partition of the subcontinent into the nation of India flanked by a divided Pakistan. Gandhi himself was murdered by a Hindu extremist. His program of nonviolence (**ahimsa**), simplicity, and economic self-sufficiency in a casteless society is but dimly remembered today, but the man himself has passed into sainthood. Any sizable Indian town boasts dozens of white- or silver-painted plaster statues and busts guarding its crossroads like gaunt ghosts, the Mahatma striding out with his wooden staff or just seated calmly in familiar pose surveying the traffic from under his godlike canopy of serpent hoods. Always freshly garlanded by some invisible hand, he now belongs to a mythic past, a time prior to the bloody partition of Mother India that wrecked his dream and well before today's mindless terrorism, communal strife, and population floods that threaten the well-being of all.

The forty-plus years since independence have seen a different balancing act, the world's largest democracy attempting to maintain a secular state with freedom for religious pluralism. Minorities such as Muslims, Christians, Sikhs, Jainas, or Buddhists feel the pressure of conformity to the dominant Hindu faith in an environ-

A common sight in every part of India is a crossroads statue of Mahatma Gandhi, staff in hand, guarded by Lord Vishnu's multiheaded cobra.

ment that assumes the identity of "Indian" and "Hindu." For their part the majority Hindus feel threatened by a government that chips away at hallowed traditions, replacing the eternal *dharma* with constitutional laws pertaining to untouchability, polygamy, divorce, inheritance, property division, *sati,* widow remarriage, dowries, and temple maintenance and revenue.

Finally, it should be noted that the modern period also witnessed the largest expansion of Hinduism outside Asia. Unlike Buddhism, which originated in India but began its spread throughout the rest of Asia within its first few centuries, Hinduism proved to be a stay-at-home faith until the medieval trading colonies were established in Southeast Asia. In the nineteenth and twentieth centuries, however, millions of Indians migrated throughout the world, as colonies of indentured laborers, merchants, physicians, engineers, and teachers creating new communities in England, Canada, the United States, the West Indies and South America, South and East Africa, Southeast Asia, and Pacific islands such as Fiji. These migrations continued in the 1970s and 1980s with burgeoning Hindu populations in several Persian Gulf states. Although Brahmans and a normal range of castes were frequently absent from new Hindu enclaves abroad, certain essentials of faith and practice remained intact. Recent temple-building activities in several second- and third-generation Hindu communities in the West are a sign of current vitality.

A separate aspect of Hinduism in the West is the development of communities and institutions ranging from the Vedanta Societies in the early twentieth century to the movements of the 1960s and 1970s, such as the International Society for Krishna Consciousness (Hare Krishna Movement), Transcendental Meditation, the ashram of Rajnish, Swami Rama, Meher Baba, the Divine Light Mission, and others.

We will return to contemporary Hinduism in chapter six. In sum, the period of the last two and a half centuries has been an era of momentous change for Hinduism as it has been for every long-lived religious, philosophical, or political system in modern global history. Hinduism as a multicultural and multiregional amalgam of traditions has been forced into a juggling act in order to keep its modernizing pan-Indian (and now worldwide) audience involved. Festival calendars; temple rituals; pilgrimage schedules; individual meditations and vows; competing Vedic, epic, Puranic, and philosophical textual traditions; *mathas*; **sadhus**; and myths must all somehow keep circulating in the air at once if Hinduism as it has been defined for the past two millennia is to continue intact into the twenty-first century.

CHAPTER IV

Dimensions in a Worldview

In the preceding brief sketch of Hinduism and the history of South Asia many details were omitted and some complex movements and traditions, many centuries in the making, were condensed to a few words of passing description. To provide a fuller treatment, this chapter will examine some of the "stuff" of Hinduism—deities, myths, texts, doctrines, rituals, sects, personalities, symbols—from the perspective of worldview, that is, a particular way of looking at and thinking about the world of human experience. Since Hinduism is rich enough in expression to afford multiple perspectives, not incompatible but interactive ones, there is opportunity to identify and explore in this chapter five different dimensions within this single worldview. In fact, Hinduism is so diverse that it may be seen as a multidimensional tradition not easily reduced to a simple code or neat system, but one that nevertheless constitutes a living whole. The term *dimension* suggests a particular extent of the tradition through the historical periods just surveyed, a range that has established enduring and essential aspects of the faith. Each of these dimensions is intrinsically Hindu, and each is dependent upon the others for its viability and coherence. Listening to the universe, mythologizing the universe, classifying the universe, recycling the universe, swallowing the universe—these are five modes of expression and therefore five zones of exploration in which to consider revelation and receptivity; myth and the significance of gods, goddesses, God, and assorted powers; being, order, function, and notions of transcendence; ritual and sacrifice; and finally, *soteriology* or the meaning of salvation. Throughout this fivefold discussion we should recognize that the diversity of Hinduism revealed in these dimensions finally gives way to coherence within a single, integrated worldview.

Listening to the Universe

> There are two Absolutes, Sound and Silence . . . Inundated by the Absolute-that-is-Sound, one arrives in the Absolute-that-is-Silence.
> *Maitrayaniya Upanishad* 6.22

If one knows when and where to be, the chanting of the Vedas may be heard daily in certain major temples, at the sites of great festivals, in Vedic schools, or in Brahman hamlets scattered about India. Brahmans who specialize in different Vedas and styles of recitation chant what they have laboriously committed to memory, one line at a time, for some eight to twenty years. Sometimes the recitant is part of a temple staff and chants to please the god during daily service. But often these Vedic Brahmans have little or nothing to do with the daily temple functions for the resident deity; they are employed by temple authorities to recite, usually between 7 and 11 A.M., simply because the Vedas should be heard in such sacred spaces.

The essential components of the Vedas are the *mantras*, timeless sounds believed to be universal and eternal. Human agents, the Brahmans, both perpetuate the *mantras* and enable others to tune in to the universe. Through them others can somehow apprehend the knowledge whose essence is *brahman*, the sacred utterance. Vedic *mantras* were and are believed to have the power to transform those who place faith in them. Since their power is cosmic they can in fact transform all the phenomena of the world. In a phrase familiar in every language of India, profound changes occur "by means of the *mantra*."

However, as we have already noted, more than two thousand years ago the great textual tradition of the Vedas began to give way to *smriti*—the Shastras, epics, Puranas, Tantras, and other texts of classical Hinduism. At the same time the great Vedic sacrifices became less important than temple and household **puja**, the worship of deities in a non-Vedic mode. Nevertheless, a sensitivity to the powers of sacred sound remains today among the most precious assets of living Hinduism. This is reflected in the continued priority of an oral over a written tradition and a reliance upon the power of *mantras*—even Tantric *mantras* and epic or Puranic verses (*shlokas*) drawn from post-Vedic sources.

During the transition from Veda to *smriti* the philosophers of the Upanishads sought to identify links between universal sound—the sacred utterance declared to be *brahman*—and the silence beyond in the realm of the unmanifest where change and distortion have no place. Such cosmic connections, they said, are revealed to one who knows. Without conscious reflection, Hindus today still express, in both individual and collective life, a variety of ways of realizing these mysterious bonds.

For comparative illustration in a single scene we are invited on a time-lapse walk for three blocks down one lane of a small town. As we begin our stroll at dawn we hear the low voice of a Brahman who recites the Gayatri *mantra* (*Rigveda* 3.62.10) in a prayer to the sun seeking wisdom and inspiration as he sips water from his palm. Later he will repeat this daily personal ritual at the other "joint" of time, twilight, as day gives way to night. Across the street another man, a shopkeeper beginning his day, reads aloud from the *Ramayana*, his daily practice. He sits on a footstool to chant the sacred text from a handsome bound volume once owned by his grandfather, who taught him to read Sanskrit. On the floor beside him sits his wife, who spends this recitation hour listening and writing over and over the name of Rama in the tiniest possible letters, filling each day the pages of a school copybook until it is completely covered with God's holy name and may then be deposited prayerfully in his temple. In midblock are two small shrines, each five feet in height and lighted by a single, bare bulb. One houses a green painted Hanuman, the other a garish orange **Ganesha**. Both are the recipients of mumbled prayers throughout the day and evening as people from every caste and social level pause before them with clasped hands.

Ahead of us at the first corner is a billboard with an improbably fashionable woman smoking a cigarette and apparently reciting Sanskrit *shlokas*. As we pass the billboard, however, we discover behind it the office and tenor voice of a lawyer who is far more involved in reciting than in disturbing any of the dusty piles of legal papers scattered about his quarters. While the other early risers have been all but inaudible, this sonorous voice would appear to be known in every corner of heaven. He hails us good morning, identifies the text that was interrupted, and says cheerfully of the list of gods and goddesses in his litany, "They are *all* good medicines and I take them every day!"

Somewhere a devotee is blowing a conch shell, either to scatter evil spirits with the sound sacred to Lord Vishnu or to awaken a deity for morning worship. As the echo of the conch fades, the heavy beat of a drum is heard from a distant lane, signaling the passing of a funeral procession on its way to the burning-ground by the river. It is the beat of Lord Shiva's drum of destruction, the end of a single human body or the end of an era of cosmic time.

In late afternoon we pass a large, old house with a group of people seated in the inner court grouped about the family priest (*purohita*), who recites a portion of the Garuda Purana. A member of the household has died, and the familiar lines about the journeys of the soul beyond this world of *samsara* are welcome sounds in this house of death and impurity. The mourners have heard the text before but do not know Sanskrit, so when the Brahman finishes his recitation he explains in the local language.

At dusk we come to the second corner and the busy temple of Shiva where a heavy traffic of devotees, three-fourths of them women, is mobile through the narrow entry gate and down the long, open corridor to the inner shrines containing the **linga** and the flanking goddesses. Accompanying the crowd, we take on a barrage of sensations: wild, lamp-lighted colors set off against the dark corners and outer hallways; splashing water; sudden cold marble against bare feet; overpowering smells of freshly spilled coconut oil and milk; thousands of fresh flowers; smoking incense, and the constant clanging of brass bells of every size, rung by each devotee to alert the many gods and goddesses of her or his arrival for worship. The bells momentarily overcome the sound of shuffling feet in the pushing throng and the murmur of prayers, but they cannot compete with the voices of priests belting out *mantra*s and *shloka*s from the tiny chambered shrines. These echoing sounds are the essence of *puja*, Vedic and post-Vedic verses in a blend of praise, devotion, and ritual attendance upon Lord Shiva, his neighboring goddesses, and all the many deities en-

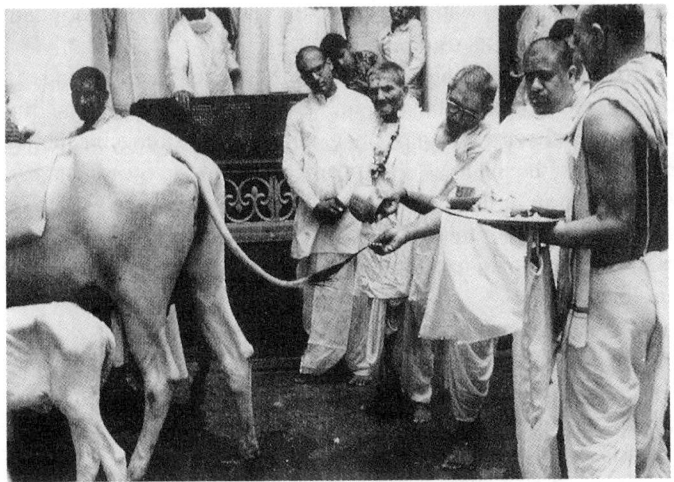

Near the conclusion of a thirteen-day funeral the chief mourner holds the tail of a cow on behalf of his deceased father and listens carefully as the priest on his left recites verses describing the cow pulling his father across the terrible river Vaitarani that separates our world from the world of the departed. Another priest pours water from the Ganges.

shrined in the outer hallways. After prayerful attention to the three interior shrines the crowd is diffused in several directions according to personal preference for continued devotions.

Small groups may be seen pressing toward any one of the thirty-odd acolyte shrines. One large shrine of Krishna and his consort Radha, here within the temple compound of Shiva, has a group of twenty-five women of all ages seated in an oval before it. They are reading aloud from the *Bhagavad Gita*, forcefully, rapidly, in a continuous presentation of the eighteen chapters. Young girls who have not yet learned the text sit among them, absorbing the mellifluous sounds of Sanskrit until they too may add their voices to the Song of Lord Krishna. As we leave the outer courtyard we see a large, pillared hall filling up with more than a hundred Brahmans and another hundred spectators, men on one side and women on the other, all gathering for a three-hour Vedic assembly to listen as learned pandits debate topics of revelation, sacrifice, *dharma*, merit and demerit, and the attainment of heaven. The pandits lace their speeches with *mantra*s and *shloka*s, addressing the crowd with the assurance of those who well know the meaning of existence and the authority of the cosmos.

It is now after midnight on our time-lapse promenade, and all the people who rise before the sun have been in bed for hours. But the deserted street is lighted by a brilliantly sparkling Hanuman temple, and the night air is bombarded with music and singing. A dozen men sit on the floor with cymbals, drums, stringed and metallic instruments, and lusty voices shouting the night away in praise of Hanuman, recounting his heroic deeds on behalf of Rama and Sita.

It is morning again, Sunday morning, as we reach the last corner of our three-block promenade, where stands a comfortable house packed with neighbors and friends crowded in to sit on the floor beside the family members. Leaving their sandals outside the door they sit reverently facing a television set garlanded with fresh flowers, incense burning, bananas and coconuts offered before it, and a lamp waved as if in the face of a god. It is time for the *Ramayana* to be seen and heard, an episode in a year-long presentation that employs the newest medium for the continuation of an age-old sacred drama.

Our short walk enabled us to hear a few of the many sacred sounds of Hinduism. Listening to the universe, as well as passing on the sacred utterances, the infinite guises of *brahman*, is a powerful form of devotion, and we realize that *shruti* and *smriti*, Veda and Purana, are inextricably blended in the *brahman*-that-is-Sound. As we noted with the woman writing the name of Rama as she listened to his cycle of tales, the passing on may also employ visual media. In fact, Hindu *mantra*s may be perpetuated in a variety of written, even iconographic forms. The Tantric tradition turned not only to esoteric sounds, mostly monosyllables, for its *mantra*s, but also elaborated ritual diagrams known as **mandalas** and **yantras** in which meditating devotees could immerse themselves as in a newly created universe. Even more common in Hinduism generally is the popular practice of writing *mantra*s on tiny bits of paper to be inserted in silver tubes or inscribing them on small copper plates, the tubes or plates then tied with a black thread around the neck, waist, or wrist of a child or adult, even at the throat of the household cow or buffalo, for protection against the evil eye, for curative purposes, or simply as an act of devotion.

In talismans and amulets the oral *mantra* continues to exert its cosmic force, usually undergirded by the shamanic powers of the religious specialist who prescribes and ties it on, just as medical practitioners from traditional Ayurvedic physicians to village spirit-healers pronounce their *mantras* for therapeutic purposes. In their own simple, unassuming way these popular and widespread mantric techniques are accomplishing the transition declared by the philosopher-poet of the Upanishads, the passage from sound to silence.

Mythologizing the Universe

> The gods entered man . . . all the gods are seated in him.
> *Atharvaveda* 11.8

Whenever one sits down to talk to people in the villages or small towns of South Asia or in the many pocket villages that try to ignore the burdens of civilization by hiding in the depths of every city, a story or two is usually forthcoming. If you are a newcomer you will need to be informed about the important events that happened on this spot to which you have journeyed. The story you hear may feature local gods and goddesses, bygone kings and heroes, power-hungry demons, weird ascetics and the beautiful women who tempted them. Everyone loves a story, particularly an old one, and "old stories," literally Puranas, are the fabric of Hinduism. It is usually difficult to separate a local tale with local characters from the vast corpus of Sanskrit Puranas. For a far-fetched parallel we must imagine dropping into an Israeli kibbutz today and hearing an old resident narrate the story of "the king's fiery furnace and Shadrach, Meshach, and Abednego, who lived in this kibbutz long ago when our ancestors were hassled by corrupt rulers." Yes, that's from the Book of Daniel in the Hebrew Bible, we say, but the narrator contradicts, "No, that's another story, not our story!"

There were, of course, "old stories," myths, legends, and folktales, already at the time when the Vedas were compiled. Their narrative force was diminished by the all-absorbing sacrifice, the attention given to compiling gigantic manuals for ritual performances and treatises probing into the meanings of sacrifice. But the good stories were never forgotten. In such great sacrifices as the royal horse sacrifice, the ashvamedha, an entire year of storytelling was demanded of the bards and singers who never failed to notice all the ways in which their king matched or exceeded the virtues and deeds of all the famous kings and heroes of past ages. It was no doubt many of these recitals, and others like them circulating in ancient India, that surfaced in the compilations of the two great Sanskrit epics and the major Puranas that were to become Hinduism's treasure house of mythology.

It is revealing that the Vedic Brahmans who recite professionally the Vedas today tell lots of good stories, but almost always they are from one of the Puranas and usually concern their special heroes, one might even say their divine prototypes, the *rishi*s. These learned Brahmans—and people in every class, caste, and stratum of Hindu society, literate or illiterate—are at home in the same universe, and that universe is thoroughly mythologized, loaded with old yet living stories.

It is the deities and demons who have long occupied center stage in Hindu mythology. The *Rigveda* and *Atharvaveda* describe on several occasions the number of gods as 33, distributed among the three levels of the universe. At the other end of the Vedic textual tradition, a passage in one of the Upanishads accounts for 33 or 303 or 3,003 gods, although the poet-theologian manipulates a clever dialogue to establish that there is in reality only one. As for the demons, the **asuras** who are presented in Hindu mythology as adversaries of the gods, these were in origin of the same order of being as the gods. A confrontation of cosmic proportions and significance between gods and demons, creation and chaos, order and disorder, righteousness and unrighteousness—in other words all that makes up the world of *dharma* against the world of *adharma* ("nondharma") is demonstrable in the mythology of South Asia, as it is in other Indo-European–speaking areas, and it remains vivid in every phase of South Asian religious history from the Vedic to the epic and Puranic periods. That gods and epic heroes can be miscreant, treacherous, even morally reprehensible, while the demons can at times be powerfully attractive, even serving as divine models for human devotees (Ravana, for example, the demon of the epic *Ramayana*, is a devout worshiper of Shiva), is one of the many intriguing features of Hindu mythology.

In the period of the late Upanishads and early epic poems, the Vedic deities who had once dominated spiritual life in ancient India—Indra, Agni, Varuna, the Ashvins, and the others—were being upstaged by just two of their number, Vishnu and Rudra-Shiva, each one of whom in time became a complex pantheon, an umbrella godhead for dozens of regional deities and cults. But the old gods did not disappear; they slipped into the background of myths, iconographies, and liturgies. Even today one finds sculptures of the ancient **lokapalas**—guardian deities at the eight points of the compass—protecting temples from their rooftop posts, although the priests, when asked, may not always be certain which is Soma, Yama, Vayu, or Agni. Brahma, the successor of Vedic Purusha-Prajapati, is remembered in countless myths as the grandfather of the gods, a kind of elder statesman among them, although one with but a single important temple active today in the whole of India. Varuna still is invoked on occasion for relief from drought, and the Ashvins for certain personal ailments, but scarce is the memory that one was once king of the gods and the twins were a first recourse in times of distress.

The sharper focus of Hindu mythology stays, as we have seen in the preceding chapter, with Vishnu and his *avatara*s (Krishna, Rama, and Narasimha in particular); with Shiva, the classical Hindu extension of Vedic Rudra; and with the many goddesses visible either as independent powers or as loyal wives of the male deities. When considering these three sets of divine manifestations centered on Vishnu, Shiva, and **Devi** (one generic name for the goddess in her multiple presences), we should not construe them as disconnected religious communities or allegiances, as for example, in the distinction between Christians who are Greek Orthodox, Roman Catholic, and Seventh Day Adventists. It is true that a "*shaiva*" worshiper pays particular attention to Shiva, a "*vaishnava*" is a devotee of one or another aspect of Vishnu (such as Krishna or Rama), and a "*shakta*" acknowledges *shakti*, feminine cosmic energy, as the motivation of the cosmos. But each pays attention to other major deities in festivals and special occasions if not also in daily prayers and rituals, and a great many Hindus express strong devotional allegiance across vaguely sectarian lines.

The very success of Vishnu, Shiva, and several powerful goddesses in Hinduism of the last fifteen to twenty centuries calls for comment. These options for the devotion of hundreds of millions of people are no arbitrary array. Instead they represent basic stirrings in the late Vedic period that coalesced in the epic and Puranic eras as tendencies to experiment with every dimension of spiritual, mental, and physiological experience, to redirect Vedic authority and institutions, and to reconceive the meaning of sacrifice and of human action in every respect. Above all, as a corrective to centuries of preoccupation with knowledge of the sacrifice as world-maintaining performance, there came into prominence a set of fundamental recognitions: this world is the realm of *samsara* or bondage to the cycle of existences; beyond this world is the state of *moksha*, release or liberation from bonds to *samsara*; though gods and God exist in the transcendent, unmanifest, unconditioned realm beyond *samsara*, they are nonetheless active *in samsara*; and the paramount means of obtaining the freedom that is *moksha* is devotion to those deities capable of rescuing the faithful.

One who seeks Krishna, who celebrates his childhood exploits, heroic battles to ward off demons and catastrophes, romantic escapades with adoring *gopi*s (milkmaids), or mystical union with Radha, his chosen one, is able to enter and relive the life cycle of Krishna through worship and meditation. And one who recounts the deeds of the ideal warrior king and hero, Rama, whose rule remains to this day the paradigm of the kingdom of righteousness and truth, participates in the mythology of another great manifestation of the same god. As Rama is the presence of Vishnu in this world, so is his wife, Sita, the feminine ideal of beauty, loyalty, and chastity, a projection of the goddess Lakshmi into this life. And again, one who sees transcendent power in Shiva, patron of wandering ascetics and *sadhu*s, employer of both passion and renunciation, lord of the cremation-ground and one whose body is smeared with ashes of the dead, is able to reconcile in the dynamic character of one deity the ambiguities and polarities of transient human as well as transient cosmic life. And the Tantric devotee who sings ecstatically his praise of the goddess and ritually elevates himself to the status of the hero, like Shiva, able to unite with her, is still another who lives out the myths and symbols spoken in a thousand ways throughout the subcontinent.

Hindu mythology is so densely forested with deities and assorted powers and so singularly lacking in discrimination about who is

Ten-armed Durga, riding her lion mount, grasps the hair of the demon king Mahisha and thrusts her spear into his side. (Durgapuja festival in Banaras)

an age-old standby and who is a recent upstart that one comes to a simple recognition that all of these deities and powers are available to anyone who wants one. An Indian anthropologist has reported from southwest India a conversation as amusingly honest as it is revealing about the changing emotional relationships between devotees and deities. Some elders had gone to the oldest temple in their village to ask the resident deity, Basava, the bull, about possibilities for rain in their drought-stricken area. Sandalwood paste, wet flowers, and bilva leaves (sacred to Shiva, whose mount is the bull) had been stuck all over the face and neck of a stone image of the reclining Basava. The elders anticipated the bull's response to their queries in a form of divination, a flower or leaf falling as a sign from the right side of his body as a "yes," from the left side as a "no." One elder stood up and addressed the deity:

> "You are famous. . . . Do you wish to retain your reputation or not? Please give us a flower. We have not performed your feast because of lack of water. . . . It has rained all around us [in the other villages]. Why has it not rained here? Tell us if you are angry. Why should

you be angry with us? We have seen to it that you do not lack anything."

A second elder contributed: "Give us your order, why do you torture us? Give it early."

The first elder, now irritated, continued: "Give us a flower on the left side if you so wish. Why do you sit still? Are you a lump of stone or a deity?"

Someone chimed in: "He is only a lump of stone; otherwise, he would have answered."

The first elder remonstrated, "We will say that there is no god in the temple and that you have left the village."

Someone else took a different line: "We are not entirely dependent upon you. On June tenth, canal water will be released by the government. . . . Even if it does not rain, we won't starve. . . . So give us a flower."

Later the anthropologist asked the villagers whether if it rained that evening (after the deity's silence), they would conclude that Basava had given the rain. They said "no." The anthropologist then asked the elders what the next step was. They said they would visit the temple on the next morning to ask for a stale flower. The priest would stand outside the door and wave lighted camphor before the deity, and everyone would wait for a flower to fall. If no flower came down then it meant that the deity had left the village.[6]

There is no doubt that the villagers believed that this deity, like all supernatural powers, could come and go in his own good time. Fields of force in this world are never stable. And in the shifting realms of multiform powers not even the line between the divine and the demonic is secure: in many of the languages of India the same word is employed for deity and demon. Nevertheless, certain figures do stand out from the crowd, as we have seen. Every village has its special deities, like Basava in the account just noted. These might be local goddesses, guardian deities, or former heroes, saints, and holy persons. Within a caste or clan there may also be gods or goddesses shared by all in the kinship group, often over an area embracing several villages, towns, or cities. Families also may consider one or another deity their special concern. Finally, at the individual level there is the particular or chosen deity, the **ishtadevata**, one among all the gods and powers with whom a spiritual bond is established, perhaps as the result of a vow or some occurrence in the vicinity of a shrine or temple of this deity. In the preceding segment, "Listening to the Universe," we noted that devotees in the Shiva temple paid attention first to the *linga* of this great god, then to personally preferred deities, perhaps those who had granted specific favors on earlier occasions, either to the devotee or someone known to her or him. In the next chapter we will observe further some of these devotional links between an individual, a family, a caste, a village, and a particular deity.

A large part of day-to-day Hindu faith and practice is spent enlisting the aid of available powers, for example, such helping or protective deities as Ganesha, Hanuman, Lakshmi, Narasimha, or Durga. Less frequently, and perhaps only through the mediation or guidance of a specialist entrusted with ominous spiritual enterprises, would there be invocations of their dangerous, often uncontrollable and malevolent counterparts, for example, the goddess Kali of the cremation- or burial-ground. But aside from pan-Indian or regional gods and goddesses, Hinduism has profound concerns for other personal powers active in a thoroughly mythologized universe, and these must not be neglected in our overview. Among them are the vaguely departed but still powerful dead, a host of amorphous demons and evil spirits, and visible or invisible celestial bodies. These too make up the everyday world of Hindu experience: ancestors, demons, and the inescapable planets.

Taking a cue from one of the earliest Vedic texts, the Laws of Manu remind all twiceborn Hindus that they have three debts to pay in this life: study of the Vedas removes the debt to the *rishis*, performing sacrifices takes care of the debt to the gods, and having sons satisfies the ancestors, the collective "Fathers," as they are known in Sanskrit. This third debt illustrates an outstanding feature of virtually all traditional societies, the powerful links, continuities, even symbiotic exchanges between the living and the dead, who are known to exist in more or less vaguely connected realms of the same universe.

Hinduism has not only vivid funerary rituals and symbols but also one of the most elaborate traditions of rituals for ancestors known to the history of religions. Those advanced into other realms from which they will later be reborn (until eventual liberation from *samsara*, the round of births and deaths) are dependent upon the living for offerings of *mantras*, food, and water. In turn, these "Fathers," including female ancestors, look out for the needs of the living. Precisely because of great detail in these ancient, still universal ceremonies, there is widespread popular concern over their absence or erroneous performance, since a troublesome spirit or ghost, possessing and otherwise interfering with the living, is the expected result if the deceased is not properly promoted and satisfied. Particularly liable to haunt the living and make special demands are all those who have died "untimely" deaths because of accidents, murders, snakebites, or other unnatural causes. Cremation- and burial-grounds, banyan trees, and other haunted places are therefore dangerous to the unwary; and the crow, who alone is able to see the formless ones, is a bird of signs and portents.

The hungry, often angry dead are not the only class of powers that threaten the living and stir caution into day-to-day existence. In fact they blend into hosts of baleful creatures that hang about the village borders, crossroads, hills, rivers, ponds, and forest tracts. In modern as in ancient India they go by many names and have almost unnumbered regional guises. Everyone knows about the night-prowling **rakshasas**, the corpse-eating **pishachas**, the mysterious **nagas** who are sometimes benevolent, sometimes deadly serpent spirits, and the fearsome haglike demoness with her feet turned backward who comes to steal away a child from the village. Humans require divine protection from things that go bump in the night, which is why every village has its guardian deity and every hamlet or city block has a Hanuman standing by with a trusty club at his side. One of the favored tales of the Puranas is stated iconographically in sculptures, paintings, and household lithographs as a seated figure with a limp body draped across its lap, looking from a distance like a pieta scene of the sorrowful mother and son. On closer inspection it is the fierce lion-headed Narasimha tearing out the guts of the helpless demon Hiranyakashipu, who once threatened his own son, **Prahlada**, for worshiping Vishnu. Such is the fate of a terrible demon, declares the icon, when he endangers the life of a true devotee of God. And such is the nature of a demon, the icon also states, that like Prahlada his good side may triumph over evil.

In another appeal to available powers, virtually everyone in India today—Hindu, Muslim, Christian, Jaina, Parsi, or even that rare new breed, the agnostic—is directly and articulately concerned with his or her relationship to the planets and their influences upon life experience. This is a matter of long tradition in the subcontinent. Offerings to the twenty-seven constellations in the lunar path are documented in the early Vedic period, and recognition of the important group of "nine planets," the **navagrahas**, is also ancient. Two of the nine planets, Rahu and Ketu, exist only in the realm of Hindu mythology, for they are connected with lunar phases and eclipses of both the moon and the sun. The others—the sun, moon, and five visible planets (a septad that provides, as it does for the Western calendar, the names of the days of the week)—are strongly mythologized, their personal influence a matter of belief quite apart from their actual appearance in the heavens. (This point also is shared with folklore and astrology in the West: most of the readers of this page know their "signs" in the zodiac, but few could locate them among the stars.) An example of the powerful hold that planets exert upon people is a pan-Indian belief in Shani, the sinister and malevolent planet Saturn. Amost every Hindu has at some point in life blamed the influence of Shani for specific failures, whether minor ones such as flunking an exam or missing a raise in pay, or such major traumas as loss of a child, a business, or sound health. And therefore virtually everyone has found time to make offerings in a shrine of the nine planets, whose images stand in a strange cluster, none facing any other, inside the compounds of temples.

One of the last of the Vedic texts, a handbook of directions for domestic rituals, concludes with a cautious reference to the nine planets: "Being revered, they revere us, but if ignored they torment us," a phrase that might be employed for *all* the named and unnamed supernatural powers of Hinduism, including most of the major deities. A person today, just like a person in India two or three thousand years ago, steps carefully into this shape-changing world, paying due respect, even worship including material offerings with prayers and *mantra*s, to the major and minor expressions of mystery, power, and the sacred. The prayerful hope is that malign powers will stand aside or be thwarted and that benevolent beings—those who reward and protect—will not abandon the village, or one's person. As the *Atharvaveda* stated long ago, the gods are all in man—or so they should be.

Classifying the Universe

Goodness, passion, inertia:
the three qualities found in material nature
bind the changeless self in the body.
Transcending these three qualities . . .
the self, freed from birth and death,
old age and sorrow, attains immortality.
Bhagavad Gita 14.5, 20

Before they retire at night or in the early morning darkness, millions of women throughout India may be seen barefoot before their houses, bent over dampened earth or pavement, creating intricate designs of white rice or lime powder. This daily feminine artistry is an ordering of the space that gives access to the family living quarters and protection of the threshold with an auspicious pattern. It is a symbolic, and therefore largely unconscious means of keeping back the "outside," the inauspicious, the impure. The designs at the borders of space are particularly important and increasingly more elaborate in the month of the winter solstice, at the borders of time as the waning half-year gives birth to the strengthening one. Nowadays mothers and daughters frequently study booklets containing designs favored in other regions of India and compete along their lanes and streets for the most spectacular continuous line drawings. These ritual diagrams are but a single example of the many ways in which Hindus organize the world of space, of time, and of all the subtle nuances of human experience.

Where space, time, and the quality of being itself are concerned the auspicious and inauspicious, male and female, inside and outside, pure and impure, hot and cool, bright and dark may all be seen as categories within a larger process of classification. Every *thing* in the universe has its niche in the great scheme of *things*; it belongs to a kind of being, separate from all other kinds of being, with certain qualities, knowable relationships, and a defined place in the hierarchy, above, equal to, or below any other specific thing.

A daughter of the household creates an auspicious design of circular green parrots at the front gate. The New Year is just beginning as she finishes.

What are the marks of this attempt to classify the universe? They are too numerous and complex to document here, but one momentous expression, older than the Vedas, has already been noted. That is a threefold hierarchy of functions—priestly, warrior, productive—evidently belonging to a Proto–Indo-European legacy refined over many centuries by Indo-Iranian nomadic pastoralists and then carried into South Asia with those who produced the Vedic tradition. This archaic principle of ordering established a determinative worldview for India: the eternal Vedas, created universe, ranks of gods, ritual fires, classes of humans, even humors within the human body, are all tripartite and hierarchic according to function. Any one of these phenomena presents itself as a unity divisible into three hierarchic but interactive constituents, that is, one supreme, one relatively devalued or even debased, and a third in mediation, active midway between the high and the low of this triadic unity.

The most famous example of this worldview is the hymn to Purusha in the tenth book of the *Rigveda* discussed in chapter two.

Purusha established the world as we know it in a definitive, cosmogonic act of self-sacrifice by projecting the dismembered parts of his person into hierarchical being. Among the parts of the world derived from this creative self-murder is human society, imagined with its classes ranked literally from head to toe as the body of God.

The quotation at the head of this segment is a continuation of this belief in the world as triadic unity. It is part of a well-known teaching of divine Krishna to the warrior hero Arjuna, one known as the *Bhagavad Gita* or Song of the Lord (Vishnu manifest as Krishna), found in the sixth book of the *Mahabharata*. Recited here is the important concept of three *gunas*, literally "threads" or "strands" of matter—constituents or qualities woven together to represent the material world. Instead of the yin-yang duality discussed in ancient China, a triad of qualities was perceived as "natural" by the philosophers of India: *sattva*, goodness, brightness, intelligence; *rajas*, activity, passion, transformation; and *tamas*, darkness, inertia, dullness. The point of Krishna's teaching is direct: these *gunas* that bind the embodied self in various combinations are all subject to change, even such apparently terminal changes feared by Arjuna and others on the battlefield, the destruction of human lives in warfare. But there is something other than these three *gunas*, beyond them, unaffected by "time" and impervious to "killing." That which Arjuna—the Indian Everyman of this sermon—must discover is the eternal *atman*, the Self identical with infinite spirit that cannot be killed.

Here the Sanskrit poetry of the *Bhagavad Gita* reflects not only the deep heritage of Vedic ritual and speculation, including the Upanishadic *atman-brahman* correspondence, but also the gradually maturing legacy of certain schools of philosophers that blossomed in the first four centuries CE. The classical systems of Vedanta, Samkhya, and Yoga actively debated metaphysics, for example, in the relationship between the world of three *gunas*, that is, nature, **prakriti**, and that which is immaterial, namely spirit or consciousness, **purusha**. Samkhya and Yoga also debated the question of a personal being or "Lord" beyond both nature and consciousness.

Appearing in the same period as the *Gita* and the developing philosophical systems was a post-Vedic medical tradition. The texts of Charaka, Sushruta, and earlier writers at the close of the first millennium BCE noted that the human body had three interactive humors, *doshas*, this triad essentially related to the hierarchic *gunas*, as well as three ranked cosmic elements: wind/air, bile/fire, and phlegm/water. This ancient tradition of medicine—Ayurveda, the Veda of longevity—is still practiced widely today throughout the subcontinent. It recognizes a healthy body as one with the three humors in balance, an unhealthy body as one reflecting imbalance. The task of this traditional medicine, and therefore of every physician, is to correct by therapy, pharmacy, diet, and advice on well-being any apparent disfunction or disharmony among these three entities. The physician focuses upon the immediate realm of qualities, humors, changes, with an eye toward a healthy "long" life in this world of *samsara*. But always there is the hint of something more. Alongside details of the gross symptoms of disease there is mention of transcendence, immutability, immortality, something beyond the constant changes of the three humors, attainable perhaps by *soma*, the ultimate pharmaceutical, or perhaps by special knowledge.

Thus the mind-set of Vedic Hinduism and the early philosophies of South Asia was prone to see the world as triadic unity. But tripartition by no means exhausted the desire to classify the universe. The number three was not the only sacred number in the spiritual calculator, nor could we expect this from the civilization that recognized 108 names of a god (not to mention 3,003 gods) and invented the digit zero in its ancient science of mathematics. Many numbers gained special status, and for many reasons. Certain integers stand out, and many of these are susceptible to hierarchic analysis.

For example, four is significant in orientation symbolism, four quarters or cardinal directions (east and west, north and south) appearing as primary components of space in the symbol systems of most world cultures. In South Asia four is also three-plus-one, gained by the addition of a subordinate or a transcendent fourth to the hierarchic triad. Thus four Vedas or four human classes, to take two prominent examples, are disclosed in the appendage of one that is both different from and less important than the original and basic three. The threefold body of the cosmic person, Purusha, is completed by the addition of feet meant to serve the upper triad of head, torso, thighs. From these feet, according to the *Rigveda*, came the Shudra class meant to serve the three twiceborn *varnas*, the Brahmans, Kshatriyas, and Vaishyas who were created respectively from the mouth, arms, and genitals of Purusha. Alternatively, a transcendent fourth is declared by superimposition of that which is above and beyond the original triad—*moksha*, for example. From the point of view of any individual in this triadic world, *moksha* deserves ultimate consideration and recognition as the designated fourth goal of human endeavor beyond *kama*, *artha*, and *dharma* (respectively, the pursuits of passion, wealth, and religious knowledge). Another example is the transcendent fourth stage (*ashrama*) of a lifebody beyond the *ashramas* of student, householder, and mendicant forest-dweller. In other words, one who has abandoned worldly goals transcends all three stages by taking a vow known as *samnyasa* and becoming a *samnyasin* (see table 4).

There are other important examples of this correspondence between the hierarchic design of the cosmos and a kind of spiritual hopscotch that is human progress. Every Vedic householder was responsible for maintaining three sacred fires that corresponded to earth (the circular domestic or preparatory fire), midspace (a semicircular defensive fire to the south), and heaven (a square fire for the essential daily offerings into the mouths of the gods). However, they are all summarized and transcended by Agni, the divine unmanifest Fire as cosmic totality. And today twiceborn Hindus still make offerings to ancestors in the manner of the late Vedic era, that is, to a sequence of three generations of deceased plus a fourth

Table 4. Examples of Subordinate and Transcendent Fourths in

Worlds	The Vedas	Purusha
4	THE UNMANIFEST	
3 Heaven	*Rigveda*	head/mouth
2 Midspace	*Yajurveda*	torso/arms
1 Earth	*Samaveda*	thighs/genitals
[4]	*Atharvaveda*	feet

assembly of remote ancestors who are envisioned now as gradually melding into the unmanifest from which they came and from which they will come again to birth and death.

Hinduism (and Indian thought in general) experiments endlessly with systems of classification. Instructive in this particular example is a lesson about the one and the many, transcendence as totality, and an Absolute discovered through perception of the twin efforts of projection and reintegration. From the unmanifest there is divulged a world—a world of qualities and experiences, ranked yet intertwined like the strands of a rope. The notion of a transcendent fourth points toward a collapse of the many and a return of tripartite creation to the primordial unity that preceded manifestation. Therefore even as the body of Purusha descended from the unmanifest as a result of the first sacrifice and the Vedas and *brahman*-as-sacred-utterance descended from silence, so is it possible for a created individual to ascend through careers of a self and the stages of a lifebody in *samsara* to the point of transcendence. Such a journey is a return to the unmanifest, the totality of being. Both the supreme identity declared in the Upanishads—that the individual *atman* is in reality *brahman*—and the later statement of *bhakti*—that the individual by devotion may become deity—are disclosed in this blueprint for cosmic and human experience.

All of this proceeds from the single illustration of the symbol of four as three-plus-one. In a similar manner classifications based on the numbers five and seven become powerful expressions in South Asian thought, that is, not only for Hinduism but also for Jainism,

Vedic-Hindu Classifications.

Varnas	*Gunas*	Life Goals	*Ashramas*
Purusha	*atman*	*moksha*	*samnyasa*
Brahmana	*sattva*	*dharma*	*vanaprastha*
Kshatriya	*rajas*	*artha*	*grihastha*
Vaishya	*tamas*	*kama*	*brahmacarya*
Shudra			

Buddhism, and most of the religions and philosophies that flourished on the subcontinent. The ritual reintegration of the cosmos in Vedic sacrifices focused upon a five-layered altar with its triadic skeleton and an *atman* as nucleus. This notion of a pentadic world body sacrificed to obtain a new and immutable body for the sacrificer (to which we will return in the next segment of this chapter) was to live on in the Upanishadic concept of five sheaths embracing the *atman* and in the important Buddhist concept of five aggregates or constituents presumed to make up an individual. The brace of cosmic elements also extended to five, namely, earth, air, fire, water, and space. Time was recognized as divisible into five seasons, gods became manifest in five successive emanations or faced in five directions, and so forth.

The extension of a triadic to a septadic symbol system was equally pervasive in Indian thought. Vaisheshika philosophy recognized not three but seven *gunas* intertwined in nature. Some Puranic cosmographies detailed seven levels in each of the three hierarchic strata of the universe and a plan of the cosmos with seven concentric continents separated by seven seas. Yoga perceived the human body as cosmos and therefore a replication of seven levels each with its point of reference, a "circle" or "lotus" as a milestone toward spiritual reintegration. Ayurveda enjoyed having it all ways: the human body is a single unit composed of three humors, five elements, five breaths, and seven substances.

Nowhere does the experimental nature of Hinduism become more apparent than in such numerological speculation. This symbolic process began with the Vedic doctrine of correspondences and an effort to connect and universalize by means of sacrifice, to regenerate every phenomenon until eventually the mysteries, the codes of creation and annihilation, could be broken and the devastating transformations of existence short-circuited. And this speculation continued with the post-Vedic philosophies, mythologies, sciences, and other symbol systems that reckoned, classified, and ranked the constituents of being and experience. The fact that both the created world and the human body undergo perpetual transformation and are simultaneously threefold, fivefold, and sevenfold poses no problem; that is no more astonishing than the fact that the two—cosmos and body—are ultimately one.

Thus we see in this third dimension explored by the Hindu tradition a recognition of enormous variations in the structure of the universe and a concomitant desire to understand and pigeonhole them. The original body of the cosmic person, Purusha, is variegated, head to toe. The world derived from his dismemberment must necessarily also be so arranged; and rank, function, order, and interdependence of members are basic facts of this world of planets, gods, humans, demons, animals, plants, and other kinds of being. The cosmos is ordered in ways accessible to the eye of faith, and knowledge of order, *dharma*, is essential for life in the world. Knowledge of the real self, *brahman*-as-*atman*, is essential for the ultimate task of summarizing and transcending the world, achieving the release from *samsara* known as *moksha*. A worldview that is forever classifying finally pinpoints synthesis and then transcendence in a category beyond all categories. "The self, freed from birth and death," according to Krishna, "attains immortality."

Recycling the Universe

> . . . the sacrifice becomes the sacrificer's Self in the other world, and the sacrificer who knows this and sacrifices in redemption obtains a new body in the other world.
>
> *Shatapatha Brahmana* 11.1.8.6

No doubt the most striking feature of Indian *society* is the class and caste system with its hundreds of isolate yet interdependent *jatis* distributed hierarchically within and beneath the classical four *varnas*. But the first distinct impression made by Indian *thought* upon the mind of the outside observer concerns the concepts of *karma* and *samsara*. In this dimension—the notion of recycling the universe—we explore further these two linked concepts that became molded into doctrines in the middle of the first millennium BCE and remained as the keystone of the South Asian worldview in every century down to the present.

The oral (eventually written) traditions that first clearly presented teachings on *karma* and *samsara* were, as noted in the second chapter, late Vedic ones, namely, the Aranyakas and Upanishads. They moved on the age-old theme of a sacrificially motivated universe, one that is perpetuated by the human work (*karma*) of *yajna*. But their authors' language was new, even radical, and their eyes were trained on a newly discovered prize unconsidered by early Vedic poets and ritualists. These new generations of poet-philosophers became a spiritual elite and vanguard of seekers of release from all births-and-deaths, not for final rebirth in the other world. What was their message and what effect did it have as Hinduism developed through successive periods of South Asian history? It is a fascinating story: the expression of "recycling" that the Upanishadic poets sought to escape has, like all things Indian, several versions.

First, we have already noted that the concepts of *karma* and *samsara* may be seen gradually evolving from the basic tenets of the Vedic worldview. Vedic faith presumed human responsibility for the ritual action (*karma*) of sacrifices that recycled cosmic energies and resulted simultaneously in continuous renewal of the world and personal regeneration of the sacrificers. An example was the famous kingship ceremony, the *rajasuya*, a great *soma* sacrifice that regenerated the principle of sovereignty and its personification on both cosmic and human scales. Order or *dharma* was directly dependent upon such renewal, and no sooner was this year-long royal consecration completed than preparations were begun to perform it all over again. The law of *karma* at that point was concise: ritual work was incumbent upon human beings, and it obtained immediate and apparent cosmic, social, and individual results. For that reason the remnant Vedic Brahman communities today still perform sacrifices. If, to take but one example, there is too little or too much rain, human and world survival hang in the balance, and among all the *karmani* (plural of *karma*) an appropriate ritual action must and can be found that is restorative.

But little in the early Vedic worldview prepares us for recognition of two notions that conjoin by the sixth century BCE. First, *karma* takes on the meaning of all action—not just ritual effort—as causal and productive of results. Second, the notion of continuing and prosperous long life in this world is no longer a worthy goal but a dilemma from which escape must be sought, a bondage to be slipped not by knowledge of the mysteries of sacrifice but by insight into the nature of a real Self that transcends this pain filled world.

This about-face of late Vedic ideology has called for explanation from historians of culture. Were indigenous peoples—whose ritual and symbol systems can be tracked as influential upon Indo-Aryan traditions early in the Vedic period—bearers of a concept of transmigration of the soul along with individual consequences of prior actions? Does a period of North Indian political, social, and economic turmoil harbor the secret of this shift from an optimistic worldview—in which an ideal life was "a hundred years and a hundred sons" and an ideal afterlife was more of the same—to a negative worldview—in which this life was defined as a burden of sorrow, a problem to be solved by a spiritual quest for release into something completely "other"?

There are no clear answers to these questions. What is obvious, however, is the lasting and commanding authority of an ideology of cycles, recycles, and earned escape from the bondage of time. Let us consider the power within this dimension by examining three motifs: the continuous sacrifice, deaths and rebirths for worlds and humans, and the eternal dance of the gods.

We begin with our previous theme of classifying the universe. The world and all its ordered categories of life are the result of a killing, the self-sacrifice of Purusha whose dismembered pieces were projected into hierarchical being and whose self-immolation became the exemplary action and destiny for all creatures who followed. The world (nature, life) itself is a temporary entity always proceeding toward its own destruction. Vedic religion was and is nothing less than a series of programmatic reintegrations and creative killings that remains continuous. Mysterious sacrifices perpetuate life as it must be in all of its diversity and multiplicity, torn limb by limb from an original unity. Systematic dismantling is not only a way of life, it is the explanation of life.

Classical post-Vedic Hinduism marks down ritual on the scale of Vedic sacrifice but it does not lose sight of the central problem: both the world and the individual human lack permanence because they are created to die. Worlds, gods, demons, humans are all mutable: only the discovered Self is without change. Does *samsara* apply to a "world"? It would appear so. The Puranas are always unfolding stories of the ages, the **yugas**, and we now live in the fourth and most wretched of ages, the Kali *yuga* (another subordinate fourth). When a world's fated time has run out, a pause will ensue and then repetition will occur "from the top," from perfection, proceeding once again down through the three hierarchic *yugas* until goodness and truth have run thin and another Kali *yuga* becomes enforced. From one point of view, therefore, world time and space are always degenerating, deteriorating, worsening. From another point of view there is "time out," a great time beyond the *yugas*, in which no thing is valued or devalued. Measurement can be only on the scale of the god Brahma himself (in the Puranas' mythic mode of semipersonalization) or on the scale of the inexhaustible unmanifest (to revert either to the Upanishads' impersonal *brahman* or the earlier sacrifice-being, Purusha-Prajapati). The time that is renewable and recyclable is the time of *samsara* for the cosmos or *samsara* for an individual lifebody in process.

But how can one make sense of *samsara* for the world? The Puranas do it quite well by opening up the mystery of "time" for mythic inspection. They display ridiculous quantities of time in myths so engaging that infinity and cyclicity seem not only plausible but entirely natural. In some Puranas a human year is but a day and a night for the gods; in others a day in the life of the god Brahma lasts for a thousand cycles of the four *yugas*, and his night is of equal duration. Since a sequence of four *yugas* lasts for 4,320,000 years, someone with an eye on the human calendar might calculate a day and a night for this geriatric deity to be 8,640,000,000 years. Brahma's relationship to the three worlds is equally fantastic, for his night is the time when an ocean overwhelms and destroys his creation, his day is the time of re-creation. In other metaphors the universe exists when he exhales or opens his eyes, and it is withdrawn when he inhales or blinks. Some Puranas employ Vishnu as creator and re-creator, Shiva as destroyer and redestroyer, with Brahma calmly balanced between, essentially above the process and yet actually the process itself. Whatever the version recited from the Puranas, the point is not lost on the devotee who listens: the world itself, like the body of Purusha endlessly collected and dismembered in the sacrifice, is a victim. And that is the glory and the peril for the human inhabitant who has yet to discover the Self that is *not* of this world.

Such accounts of astronomical time spans lead one to think of sameness in eternal recurrence. But repetition, recycling, does not always mean sameness. The ancient Vedic sacrificer (or his modern counterpart) sacrificed every day, that is, he offered milk into the household fire in the ritual known as *agnihotra* at dawn and twilight, at the joints of time as it were. Occasionally, however, he also performed extraordinary sacrifices, rituals that required as much as a year or two to complete. By the same token the modern Hindu may bathe every day in the river at Allahabad (formerly Prayaga, one of a triad of Hinduism's ancient sacred cities including Kashi [Banaras] and Gaya), where three great rivers are joined, namely the Ganga, Yamuna, and the invisible subterranean Sarasvati. But on a certain day he or she will be accompanied by a million others because of a particular joint in time, that is, a special astrological conjunction. Like the Vedic sacrificer who achieves exceptional status from performing a great *yajna*, this simple pilgrim of today is spiritually transformed in the presence of uniquely auspicious temporal and elemental mergers. Literally "things have come together" for the bather, as indeed for the sacrificer, and life can proceed with new momentum.

The modern cosmopolitan view of human existence declares on its best current evidence that we are mobile organisms on a spheroid spinning on its axis while it orbits a much larger spheroid that itself is a speck inside a vast gaseous mass traveling at vertiginous speed away from an unknown point in the cosmos. It is a story upon which few can focus for more than a couple of minutes at a time; we are, after all, busy being mobile organisms. Hindus have trouble focusing on *their* myths of *samsara* for the world or the individual: they too are preoccupied mobile units inside families, clans, castes, villages, and regions. It is common belief, however, that each lifebody is engaged in a long sequence of births-deaths-rebirths in this world. In the next chapter we have occasion to track an individual lifebody along a unique passage through a shared series of events in one episode between conception and death.

The notions of what happens between death and conception in another womb, however, call for discussion here, since they illustrate key articles of Hindu belief. Like birth/rebirth, death is a dangerous period of transition and therefore one of significant impurity for the entire family. One emergent from a womb enters this world like an immigrant; one who exits from a lifeless body is therefore like an emigrant off on a journey . . . once again. Classical texts attempting to capture this thought of a soul traveling from body to body employ such metaphors as a caterpillar crawling from leaf to leaf or a person changing old for new clothes. But it is ritual manuals that provide us with many intriguing details about the transitions and how they are accomplished. As in other traditional cultures, India reveals not only continuities between the living and the dead but also symbiotic duties, that is, mutually beneficial actions. It is the living who promote the deceased with food, water, and *mantras*, while the advancing ancestors look out for their descendants from the vantage points of their otherworldly station.

One who dies must be established ritually as an ancestor, a *pitr*, literally, a deified "Father," for such powerful status does not happen automatically with the loss of a body. Traditionally this requires ten days of rituals, representing, perhaps, like the ten days of rituals immediately after childbirth, the ten lunar months of developmental residence in the womb, growth and acclimatization in a new environment. One is not fully human at birth, one is not fully ancestral at death: in both cases ritual efforts are necessary to refine a being and eliminate its defects. Part by part a temporary and invisible body is fashioned in ten days, enabling the deceased spirit to cross over and join the safe company of preceding ancestors of the lineage. Frequently, shortened versions of these rites prevail, but in any case the ancestors—including this newly arrived member—require continued attention, particularly on new moon days and death anniversaries. That attention is primarily in the form of cooked rice ritually offered.

The sense that after three generations ancestors begin to dissolve into vaguer zones from which they are eventually reborn is present in the texts discussed today by priests and scholars. In the Upanishads two celestial paths for the dead were distinguished, one of the gods and another of the Fathers (ancestors). The former path leads by way of the moon to the world of *brahman*, the Absolute, and is for those who do not return to terrestrial births. The latter path, linked to a schedule of sacrifices, recycles beings to the world of rebirths. As noted, the *Chandogya Upanishad* describes the return journey by way of the moon back into earth in rain, growth as a plant that is soon eaten, and then rebirth from the womb of the eater, human or animal, according to the *karma* of the eaten. Even older texts such as the *Shatapatha Brahmana* related the mystical development of a cosmic self-body by meditative means and ascetic techniques (**tapas**, the practice of creative austerities), both as expressions of sacrifice. In this way mind, speech, breath, vision, hearing, action (*karma*), and fire are successively generated by knowledge. It is important to note that despite all the changes Hinduism has undergone in the past twenty-five or twenty-eight centuries since those texts were composed, the connection between human ritual activity and the recycling of the dead has never been broken.

But other concerns intersect with this ancient and still pervasive ritual one. For example, since the Vedic period the deceased is said to return to the elements in a reversal of creation, that is, the original projection of Purusha-Prajapati's body into cosmic being is turned about. Breath returns to wind, the eye to the sun, hair to the trees, and so on, the assumption being that after an interval the elements will once again be reassembled in the form of a human body. We are reminded that Prajapati is exhausted after his effort of creation, that the three worlds are exhausted each time the curtain comes down on the Kali *yuga*; it would seem that an individual self too has the right to be exhausted between births, between "actions." For the individual, *karma* is not dissolved but carried along to remain effective—even determinative—as long as existence in *samsara* is continued. The remarkable point is that from the time of the Upanishad Hinduism's stated target for the self is *moksha*, that termination of all future rebirths and location of the self on a path of the gods from which there is no return. And yet replenishment and reconstitution come in the form of food from the living in order to promote and recycle, not to liberate, those emigrant dead.

Here is one of the fundamental paradigm shifts of Hinduism. The ancient Vedic desire to "hold on" to the dead, the forefathers, as recorded in the citation at the head of this segment is a natural human one: a new, ritually created and therefore immutable body awaits the deceased in the other world. Continuing anxiety about "redeath" and dissolution of that self-body, however, reflects not a lack of faith in ritual action, but rather an uncertain belief in the efficacy of sacrifice *in the other world*, that is, the world of the Fathers. In the logic of *karma* as ritual work/action, recycling the dead for yet another chance would satisfy both the human need to keep one's fathers and the ethical requirement to improve the fathers' spiritual report cards, even to the point of divine graduation. And so an ambiguity that remains to this day was written into Hindu faith and practice in the middle of the first millennium BCE: the living feed their forefathers as if they were gods in heaven in order to bring them back to earth as humans.

Another item on the agenda of this committee of the living and the dead has to do with debts to be paid. As we noted above in the segment on mythology, it is believed that everyone enters the world carrying three debts, one to the *rishis*, to be paid off by reciting *mantras* (Vedas); a second to the gods, to be settled by offerings to them; and a third to the ancestors, to be reckoned by bearing children and thereby continuing the lineage. Those three are identified already in early Vedic texts. But throughout India today many Hindus wish to select their parents from the collective ancestors and assign to them a special payment, often in the form of a long pilgrimage to a sacred city such as Gaya or Nasik, where lengthy rituals may be performed on behalf of this recently departed pair.

A final point regarding this complicated journey of the emigrant, soon-to-be-immigrant dead is that of reward and punishment in other realms. Descriptions of heavens—such as Vishnu's, named Vaikuntha—and hells—the stratified Narakas—are famous in Hindu mythology, and the Puranas delight in lurid details, sometimes with more precision on the side of torment than bliss. The symbolic sacrifice-gift of a cow during postcremation rites, for example, has a precise purpose. The deceased's spirit may then grasp the tail of this beneficent creature as she swims across the dread river Vaitarani, a thick stream of pus, blood, and sweat into which the soul might otherwise descend in suffering because of past evil deeds (see photograph on page 79). The *karma* system of automatic retribution might appear to be a just and sufficient reading of the balance sheet of an individual's accumulated merit and demerit during each successive rebirth. But a series of temporary residences in situations of pleasure or pain becomes an added guarantee of attention to action on the part of the living, lest they too sink in the Vaitarani River with no cow's tail to the rescue.

There is another intriguing aspect of cyclicity revealed in the mythologies and iconographies of gods and goddesses who dance—Krishna, Ganesha, Virabhadra, Kali, and others. Like musicians, dancers keep time and expose the fluidity of past, present, and future. Nataraja, "Lord of the dance," is an epithet of Shiva, and earlier we listened to the beat of a funerary drum that served as reminder of Shiva's cosmic dance of destruction. At his temple in Chidambaram in Tamil Nadu a multi-armed Shiva can be seen dancing on one foot within a ring of fire, his matted locks flying, the drum in his upper right hand balancing a flame of destruction in his upper left hand, a lower hand pointing toward his foot that has risen gracefully free of this world, and an opposite hand gesturing peacefully "fear not" to the worshiper. A devotee's eye cannot escape being drawn through this energetic symmetry to the serene and meditative face of the divine. The Lord's dance has been going on for eternity, according to a local Purana concerning this temple, and is praised in the Vedas—although even they do not understand its significance. When the forest could not withstand the awful vibrations of his dance, Shiva continued to the beat of his drum within the great hall of Chidambaram. His mysterious "space

Stacked here to conclude a hundred-day ritual for Nataraja (Shiva as Lord of the Dance) in his temple at Chidambaram, Tamil Nadu, are 2,016 clay pots. Half the pots are white, representing Shiva, and half are red, for his consort, the goddess Shivakamasundari. A hundred priests conduct fire sacrifices at nine surrounding altars. (Photo by John Loud)

linga," also at the heart of this temple, is one of the five elemental Shiva *lingas*—earth, water, wind, fire, space—distributed in five famous temples of South India. Thus the "outsider" god became an "insider" where he may be worshiped in the invisible form of his powerful generative phallus and where he points the way to liberation from the world that his dance is even now destroying.

In many cases it is not the god alone who dances but a human possessed by the god. God-dancers, exorcists, or shamanlike healers can be possessed by Shiva, for example, or by one of his terrifying *avataras* such as Bhairava or Virabhadra, and dance ecstatically for many hours. In such cases channels are open to that otherness frequented by Shiva, including the realms of demons and ghosts of the untimely dead.

Another well-known dancer is Krishna, whose **lila** ("sport, play") with the cowherd girls (**gopis**) in the moonlit forests of Vrindavana by the Yamuna River is one of the most cherished episodes in all of South Asian literature. Celebrated by medieval poets, painters, sculptors, and musicians, this dance—a circular one, like time—is another world-abandoning one, although the Krishna *lila* is nuanced not with fire and destruction but by all the charming interplay of romantic love, even erotic detail, the bliss of union, sexual jealousy, and the anguish of separation. In the tenth book of the *Bhagavata Purana* the Sanskrit poet reveals the scene: amorous *gopis* have forsaken their household duties, including their husbands and infants and, lured by the magic of Krishna's flute, have run off to the forest to seek him. To assuage the competitive jealousies of the *gopis*, Krishna extends his divine grace to these souls who have renounced *dharma* out of devotion to and desire for him and multiplies himself so that each may dance with the god in a great whirling circle of bliss.

This Gopala (cowherd) Krishna theme of the Sanskrit Puranas, the Sanskrit *Gita Govinda* (in which Krishna's favorite *gopi* is identified as Radha), and the vernacular poets of *bhakti* in nearly every region of India continues by means of the motif of *lila* an important earlier article of faith. In the third chapter of the *Bhagavad Gita*, Krishna declares to Arjuna that he has nothing whatever to accomplish in the three worlds, nothing that he should attain. "And yet I continue to act," admits the god, so that "these worlds will not perish." In other words, Krishna's *karma* is like that of the

Vedic sacrificer insofar as it is action that regenerates cosmic energies. But from the wider context of the *Bhagavad Gita* his counsel is clear: his action is a model for Arjuna and therefore all humans, for it is detached action, with no thought for personal rewards or the fruits of action. This is of course the meaning of play or sport, the *lila* that has no end in view, the dance in the moonlit forest that is freedom from the world of contingencies and the ordered, classified world of *dharma*, not to mention the continuous sacrifice.

And again, there is another dark dancer, the fearsome goddess Kali, black as night, her blood-red tongue lolling, the dismembered limbs of human victims jangling at her waist as she prances on the pallid, inert form of her consort Shiva. She is *shakti*, feminine cosmic energy, dancing another message, a lesson on the transient nature of everything and everyone, including even Mahadeva, the great god Shiva. Hers is the power of creation, and in the bowl of food she offers with one hand she proves that she is the Mother of all life. Raised in her other hand, however, is the bloody sword of decapitation, and there she discloses the incontestable brevity of life for all her creatures in this world.

Thus three dancers, varied as their choreographies and rhythms may be in myths, poems, and iconographies, perform on the same stage of world and human experience.

In an earlier segment, "Classifying the Universe," we noted that one of the many ways of ordering experience that is meaningful to Hindus is the separation of that which is pure from all that is impure or polluted. The interplay of purity and pollution, like that of harmony and disharmony or projection and assimilation, is yet another example of the Hindu cyclical view. To the outside observer of the overpopulated Indian landscape many rivers are sewers choked with refuse, feces, industrial effluents, and not infrequently the corpses of animals and humans. To the Hindu insider every river is sacred and eternally pure, the element of incorruptible power in which one is cleansed inside and out by drinking from and bathing in this fluid goddess. How can this be when Hindus are so concerned with the pollution of bodily wastes, hair, animal skins, and everything reminiscent of death? The answer must lie somewhere in the profound recognition that cosmic energies and elements are renewable resources, that the universe is driven by perpetual regenerations, and that in the final analysis it is a process of necessary and repeated dying that mysteriously provides new being for the world, its elements, and its inhabitants of every species.

By tracking a fourth dimension in this chapter we have located another way in which Hinduism has been constantly innovative yet consistent with its earliest sense of direction. The sacrifice that provided "the first cosmic laws" is still in action, and continuous. The cosmic dance of the god and goddess is still in action, and continuous, "lest these worlds perish." And the births and deaths of each of us are still in action, and continuous. We are in fact defined by our actions, all of them, until the final bonds of ignorance and attachment are broken and the sacrifice-dance of these worlds is absolutely of no consequence.

Swallowing the Universe

> The true yogi meditates, realizing
> . . . I am a stranger to this world,
> there is no one with me!
> Just as the spume and the waves
> are born of the ocean then melt back into it,
> so the world is born of me and melts back into me.
>
> *Yoga Darshana Upanishad* 10.6[7]

The cartoon stereotype of an Indian ascetic portrays an emaciated fellow in a loincloth lying flat out on a bed of spike nails. Occasionally at festivals or pilgrimages in the carnival-like atmosphere outside renowned temples, one may see this and other bizarre examples of self-mortification. The true ascetics of Hinduism, however, are not performers and claimants of small coins but large-scale explorers, dedicated and intrepid seekers, occasionally solitary, usually social, often pushing out the limits of human endurance in body, mind, and soul. Asceticism can take the form of the ordinary housewife who decides to fast for two days as a particular vow (**vrata**); a wandering mendicant who for decades walks from village to village as a holy man; or the *yogi*, practitioner of *yoga*, who works toward the cessation of normal thought processes by first altering normal respiration, blood pressure, diet, and other physiological routines.

A Tantric yogi *in red garments meditates deep underground in a womblike shrine of the black goddess Kali. Flanking her jeweled image are human skulls and the wooden sandals of former* gurus *on the Tantric path.*

Paleontologists and marine biologists inform us about "minimal organisms" that dominated the fossil record of life on earth half a billion years ago and still exist today as tiny animals—brachiopods and stalked crinoids, for example—in the depths of the oceans. Their consumption of oxygen in relation to body weight is the smallest of all animals, and this low metabolic rate makes them the most efficient of organisms. If we were to imagine a model for the *yogi* we might suggest such minimal organisms who are in but not of this world, barely functional in the eye of busier, more ambitious creatures, but destined nevertheless to survive the changes that signaled extinction for millions of species. The brachiopod and the *yogi* are survivors because they have conquered the dangerous process of change; each has perfected a technique of absorbing an entire world of change.

The *yogi* is an outward sign of a final dimension taken by Hindu tradition, one demonstrated time and again over three millennia of myths, rituals, doctrines, and symbols until it has become one of the fundamental components of the worldview. It is a reflection of physiological and mental experimentation, spiritual audacity, profound intuition, stubborn courage—and even sporadic humor and incredulity—that enabled certain movements in South Asia to promote and to realize in spirit so immodest a goal: the swallowing of the universe.

In a Vedic *soma-yajna* known as the *vajapeya*, the sacrificer swallows the drink of strength (*soma*), places his foot on the sacrificial pole that connects the three worlds, and in triumph announces "I have become immortal." Clearly, spiritual modesty was not the medium of Vedic faith. Even a student of the Vedas, proclaims the *Atharvaveda*, seizes the three worlds and brackets the seas, repeatedly fashioning them. As knower of Vedas and as future sacrificer the student will transcend change by identifying the precise ritualized killing that extinguishes imprecise dying. And the Upanishads, as we have seen, make a quantum leap with a discovery that even the killing can be sacrificed, that is, forfeited. Indeed it must be given up, because the animal or *soma* sacrifice itself is action that binds the sacrificer. The Upanishadic poet-philosopher locates the ultimate liberating audacity "Everything is *brahman*, *atman* is *brahman*, I am *brahman*."

This aggressive spirituality of Vedic tradition was not limited to the sacrificer and his cohorts. There is an equally bold legacy of the heroic warrior, from mythologies of an intrepid Indra in the *Rigveda* to the militant energies of Kshatriyas, who taught the new Upanishadic mysteries to educated but unenlightened Brahmans. The notion of action as courageous, heroic physical force that defined the Indo-European warrior lived on in the Indian epics, classical and medieval. More important, it endowed South Asian spirituality at large with this enduring concept: transformation occurs in the mediating, connecting midspace or midtime. That passionate midspace is the liminal realm not only of Indra, Arjuna, and other heroic warriors of mythic and epic fame, but also of the *avatara*s who appear as saviors in times of human and cosmic crisis. Again, it is the territory of *rajas*, the connecting link in the triad of the *guna*s.

Midspace is thus the pause in the laborious process of creation, but also the pause in an equally stressful return journey, a process of reintegration that is world-and-self-destructive, but Self-locative. The "heroes" (*viras*) of Tantrism see themselves as bold warriors of the middle ground, between the trenches, as it were, of domesticity and bondage behind, transcendent unity still ahead. Examples of such mediation are found outside Hinduism as well. There are the *bodhisattvas* and *buddhas* of Mahayana Buddhism, those who postpone their earned *nirvana* and challenge *samsara* until it is defeated for all beings. And there are the *tirthankaras* or *jinas* of Jainism whose conquest of the self is one of cosmic proportions.

There were and still are many figures on this no-man's land, those who followed the beat of a different drummer: long-haired ascetics who ride on the wind, go naked or clad in dirty red loincloths, and drink with Rudra a cup of "poison" are described in the *Rigveda*. Their traditions date at least from the late second millennium BCE and could well be much older; but since they left us no texts, of such ascetics we know only what little the Vedic poets and ritualists cared to relate. Other communities such as the Vratyas, ancient bands of pastoral nomads known in the *Atharvaveda* for their special vows, sacrifices, sorcery, and prowess in ritualized warfare—all apparently at variance with the norms—may have generated certain legacies of ascetic techniques.

The middle of the first millennium BCE brought greater visibility to ascetic traditions and linked them to concepts of renunciation already evident in Vedic articles of faith, for example, in the vows of the Vedic student, the *brahmacarin*; in the ritual consecration, **diksha**, undertaken by the sacrificer; and the formula of *tyaga* or renunciation pronounced by the offerer who abandons to a deity the fruits or results of sacrifice. A common rubric for certain counter-Vedic communities of this period—the Ajivikas, Jainas, and Buddhists who rejected the authority of the Vedas and the *dharma* of class, caste, and sacrifice—is *shramana* movements. The *shramana* is a "striver," one who exerts himself or herself as a renunciant mendicant on the path to liberation from *samsara*. Early on these movements established monastic orders of monks and nuns. While the Buddhists emphasized a middle path between rigorous ascetic techniques and self-indulgence, the Jainas were steadfast adherents to progressively severe regimens of self-mortification (*tapas*) and maintained, even to the present day in its conservative sect, the vow of nudity for monks.

The Upanishads synthesized and to a certain extent institutionalized renunciation in the schedule of four *ashramas*. As we have noted, an ideal triadic program—student, householder, forest dweller—is capped by a transcendent fourth life-stage entered through the vows of renunciation taken by the *samnyasin*. In abandoning the three worlds the renunciant virtually swallows the three ritual fires, that is, interiorizes them and discontinues all prescribed external offerings. One who has taken *samnyasa*, a vow that ideally eliminates all the principles by which the world of *dharma* is classified, including class, caste, and ritual status, is transcendent yet still involved. That is a powerful but necessarily ambiguous model. The renunciant is one deserving of liberation but still living, and in that respect is a Hindu counterpart to the *bodhisattva* of Mahayana Buddhist tradition. Pointing toward a difficult but not impossible ideal, the role is there as a measuring stick; in practice there are few who embrace entirely the renunciant path. The *sadhu*, *yogi*, holy person, and realized saint all take their cue from this concept of liberation from *dharma* typified by the *samnyasin*. And all are burdened by the ambiguity of the Vedic sacrificer who "abandons" what is sought and the *samnyasin* who keeps what was abandoned. Still continuing today is the institutional process begun twenty-five centuries ago by the establishment of the third and fourth *ashramas* and by the counter-Vedic *shramana* movements. In 1987 a pan-Indian society of *sadhus* decided to publish a "national directory of eminent holymen of the country," thus assuring a continuing professionalization of such figures who presumably have renounced worldly professions.

Their expressions are manifold. In chapter three we have already seen two examples in Yoga and the Tantras. The *Bhagavad Gita* disparages the idea of asceticism but stamps with approval a special kind of renunciation. Inaction is not possible, says Krishna to Arjuna, with reference to asceticism, for a *yogi* in transic concentration, like a tortoise with limbs drawn inside its shell, is still an actor bound by the activity of being. But sacrifice or abandonment of the fruits of action—that, says Krishna, is the correct path. Detached action is thus a compromise, a legitimation of the householder's life-style over against the renunciant who abandons family and society. The *Bhagavad Gita* thus adds its teaching to a longtime tension in Indian culture between the abandonment of desire for the world and the desire to conquer the world by embodying it.

Another aspect of this same tension between abandonment and conquest involves gender symbolism. As in other areas India has it all ways: the female is both elemental matter (*prakriti*) that traps masculine spirit (*purusha*), and therefore a negative force, or exactly the reverse, a positive force as intelligence or wisdom that liberates. Similarly, the human soul can either be female in love with the male deity (Krishna) or male in self-sacrificing submission to the female deity (Durga or Kali). Either way the deity wins and the world, including its two temporary genders, loses. Deities are frequently manifest in what the world labels inappropriate gender—Siva as the god who is half female, Siva incarnate as a female Vishnu (Mohini), the goddess Durga as heroic lion-riding warrior, the renowned warrior Arjuna disguised as a transvestite—and in the end the deity may often declare both genders and also genderlessness. And so we are turned back by these myths, iconographies, and rituals upon the inexpressible and qualityless *brahman* as Absolute.

In a remarkable way the traditions of the Tantras in the middle of the first millennium CE perpetuate a discovery declared a thousand years earlier in one of the Upanishads: the world can be absorbed and dismissed by the union of the two genders, and feminine cosmic energy or intelligence is an active, liberating force. Thus the goal of world abandonment was eventually declared attainable by a dangerous path, that of indulgence rather than renunciation.

The Tantric schools of *yoga* evolved as secret counter-ascetic communities bent on release by extreme actions. These actions included, as we have seen earlier, ritual performance of the "five M's," one of them, *maithuna*, being either symbolic or actual sexual union. From one point of view the Tantric *yogi* embracing his young, low-caste, female-as-goddess partner is performing the most outrageous breach of religious law in this adharmic (anti-*dharma*) behavior, overturning Hinduism's traditional display of celibacy as spiritually meritful. From his point of view, however, he has left *dharma* behind and is pushing the limits toward androgynous union and a genderless territory of origins/conclusions. In fact he insists that for him, a *vira* (hero) like Shiva, the sexual act is not a lack of continence but precisely a demonstration of cosmic self-control. Unlike domesticated, nonheroic creatures who procreate and die, he does not suffer semen loss. Like the Vedic sacrificer reversing Purusha-Prajapati's dismemberment/creation and returning to the moment before creation, he intends by his counter-ascetic action to reverse time and locate the moment of primordial unity. His recognition of the goddess as *shakti* is multiform: he worships her, is empowered and liberated by her, and finally embodies and transcends her.

He tells us all of this in his cryptic texts and vivid practices. For example, according to Hindu physiology semen is life-essence and properly belongs at the top of the head. In Tantric Yoga the top of the universe and the top of the head are one, as indeed *soma* and semen are one. *Soma* descends in time and space and worlds are continually born anew; semen descends in the body and is lost in the procreative act that perpetuates birth and death in the world. The Tantric *yogi* reverses this natural, worldly, human flow: semen is not ejaculated but directed upward through the channels of the body, even as feminine cosmic energy, *shakti* or **kundalini**, roused from its coiled and serpentine sleep on the feminine earth, ascends from its locus beneath the navel. Unity of these two—white masculine essence and red feminine energy, deified respectively as Shiva and Shakti—is achieved in the thousand-petaled lotus in the crown of the body-become-universe.

In the words of the text cited at the head of this segment "the world is born of me and melts back into me." The creation, absorption, then re-creation of the cosmos, a cycle detailed so well in the Puranas, has become an interior event for this *yogi* who reports about **samadhi**, his state of total reintegration, fulfillment, and interiorization. The three main channels within his body are ruled, he says, by Shiva, Vishnu, and Brahma, while such Vedic gods as Prajapati, Varuna, Vayu, Soma, Pushan, and Viraj protect other conduits for vital breaths and fires (just as these Vedic gods are found today in the concrete form of strategically placed guardian deities in Hindu temple architecture). The courses of the sun and moon, as well as their eclipses, and the changes of the seasons all take place within the *yogi*'s body, and therein are the meetings of the holy rivers, the cosmic mountain Meru, and the sacred city of Banaras. No need for a pilgrimage to Banaras if it is embodied, no need to offer to the gods if they are within, no need for a clock or a calendar if world time as well as world space are the Self.

Obviously the dimensions of Hinduism discussed above are all encompassed by this new one: the world that is listened to, mythologized, classified, and recycled is also the embodied world, the swallowed world. In the eleventh chapter of the *Bhagavad Gita* there is a famous theophany in which Arjuna's charioteer reveals himself to be not only Lord Krishna but the transcendent Vishnu, godhead behind all gods. Krishna supplies heroic Arjuna with a divine eye so that he may bear, if only briefly, the splendor and terror of this vision with the light of a thousand suns. "The whole universe," announces Krishna-Vishnu, "is united inside my body." And Arjuna, witness to the very process of reintegration, is struck dumb at the sight of gods, sages, demons, ghosts, humans, animals all in a great white-water river rushing into the multiple flaming mouths of this awesome god as if to the sea. The sea is Krishna is Vishnu but yes we now know it as Purusha as we recognize through Arjuna's eye the raging torrent of *samsara.* All one body we. Food for the god.

But what of swallowers today, what of the living sadhus, saints, god-men, *samnyasi*s, *yogi*s, who challenge the comfortable norms or quietly pass on their traditions in *math*s, *ashram*s, or the million roads of India? Clearly they have multiple roles and are as diverse a lot as the strivers and questers of ancient times.

In the same region of South India are two opposite examples, one the passive, silent, lonely seeker, like the tortoise with all its limbs drawn in, said to have renounced not only society but also food. He is Bal Yogi, who lives in a cave on a hillside. Believers swear that he emerges on only one day of the year to eat in silence a modest ball of cooked rice offered to him by a devotee. If they are correct, then he is even more efficient an organism than our example of the brachiopod. The other is Sathya Sai Baba, one of India's best known god-men, easily recognizable on calendars and posters all over India by the Afro hairstyle framing his smiling, well-fed face. In no way does he resemble a traditional *yogi,* and he is certainly no brachiopod. Now in his late sixties, he continues to dispense holy ash (*vibhuti*) and the sight (**darshana**) of his person as a living, breathing *avatara* of the divine to hundreds of thousands of devout believers and fascinated onlookers every year. Having cured himself publicly in

1963 of an incapacitating illness (described variously by the faithful as a heart attack, paralytic stroke, or tubercular meningitis), Baba is seen by many to have miraculous healing powers for any believer who is ill or disabled. Locally, in the Telugu-speaking vicinity of his ashram at Puttaparthi, Andhra Pradesh, he is known by all classes and castes, but his pan-Indian appeal is particularly to those of the urban middle class who have followed his cult in newspapers and magazines for four decades as he flies from Bangalore to Delhi, Bombay, or Madras, or tolerates the reverent Americans and Europeans who sit at his feet.

Like the Tantric *vira* (hero) Sathya Sai Baba identifies with Shiva, and like the *yogi* in the Yoga Darshana Upanishad he embodies all gods and goddesses as well as the cosmic unison of Shiva and Shakti. Tantrism and ascetic *yoga,* however, have no place in this cult that highlights a *guru*-as-god. Baba explains his relationship to this world in the traditional mode of the *avatara,* that is, as a god who engages with the world in times of crisis and need. In fact, he claims to be a tripartite *avatara* of past, present, and future. First he was the famous Sai Baba of Shirdi in Maharashtra, western India, dispensing Shiva's holy ash until his "death" in 1918; now he is Shirdi Sai Baba's reincarnation in Andhra; and he will come again a third time as Prem Sai, in yet another state of modern India, Karnataka.

In Sathya Sai Baba and similar figures today we see a demonstration of the deity-become-human, the being who is as free to return to the world as he is to swallow it. For the many devotees who see him as Bhagavan, the Lord, and as omniscient, clairvoyant miracle worker, he is the God of our time and our place. The fact that these believers are involved in education, social service, medicine, disaster relief, and other varieties of institution building indicates they intend neither to abandon the world nor identify with Baba. He is an *avatara,* a sufficient manifestation, and a relevant ideal in an imperfect age. More than this, he is a target of devotion, and it is precisely because he has entered the world and transformed their lives that his followers cannot imagine leaving it.

Not all are believers who see or hear about Sathya Sai Baba's favorite act of pulling packets of sacred ash or wristwatches out of thin air. Some are scoffers, and they also represent a tradition of Hinduism. Many ascetics, *sadhu*s, self-proclaimed *guru*s, and divinely realized saints have a hard-core following of disbelievers, those who dismiss them as charlatans, snake-oil salesmen, or just false-faces for a degenerate age. But many, on the other hand, would accept the statement of a government clerk in response to a scholar's query about ascetics today: "A *sadhu* has a deep understanding of life's philosophy and believes in god. *Sadhu*s are the force that keeps society going."[8]

Swallowing implies eating, digesting, the processing of food, and these are among South Asia's favored metaphors. The *Taittiriya Upanishad* contains a famous passage concluding with the chant *aham annam aham annam aham annam* (I am food I am food I am food). It reminds the hearer of the chain of being in which each individual in *samsara* has been recycled to earth in rain, emergent as plant, eaten as someone's food, born as embryo, grown into eater of food, but only for a moment until the eater is once again the eaten—*aham annam*.

Revealed in the five dimensions explored in this chapter is a diversity that is astonishing given that all of our probing has been within a single religious tradition. Listening, mythologizing, classifying, recycling, swallowing the universe—these appear like experimental balloons sent up to try the currents of the wind and determine possibilities. No doubt other balloons have soared well enough across the early Vedas, Upanishads, Yoga Sutras, epics, Puranas, Tantras, medieval devotional poets, and beyond. Finally, however, the diversity of Hinduism disclosed by these experimental flights appears to give way to coherence within a single worldview.

It is as if each experiment were able to intuit the mobility of all the others and locate a common flight pattern. As we have seen, a tendency to effect compromises has assisted in this remarkable coordination. When ascetic movements contest the standards, asceticism is given latitude and legitimacy. When indulgence is proposed as an alternative to austerity, it is ritualized and declared a gateway to liberation. The message is, strive to perform one's proper duty in society; but also, strive to abandon the world—or at least the fruits of action. In the same period in which Shankara extols absolute nonduality and *brahman* without qualities, Manikkavachakar praises and confesses, laughs and weeps before his Lord sweet as honey. All gods, one God, no gods, multiple solutions. The inexhaustible Vedas, compact Sutras, favorite Puranas, dynamic epics, poems of local saints in the local language—all are sacred, all are essential, and no one of them is sufficient for everyone. Thus the paradox of Hinduism: experiments appear to have no limitation, yet none is so radical as to fracture the mold.

The five dimensions surveyed above do express this seemingly limitless yet coordinated participation in the Hindu worldview. Taken in the order in which they were discussed they provide a summary of Hinduism: the oral tradition is mythology concerning classifications in a world of *samsara* that can be transcended.

In chapter one a typical Hindu was identified as one who would accept *karma* and *samsara* in the belief system, uphold certain sacred texts and deities, honor ancestors with a continuing lineage and with offerings, admit to class and caste status within a broader social system, express certain overt or symbolic ascetic practices such as fasts or vows, and consider important the pursuit of goals toward ultimate release. In the process of reviewing five dimensions of the Hindu worldview we see that all of these aspects of identification are between twenty-five and thirty-two centuries old. It is the task of the next chapter to engage with some of the dynamics of contemporary faith and further probe the range and effectiveness of this singular worldview.

■

CHAPTER V

The Dynamics of Hinduism

So far Hinduism and history have been surveyed as well as some of the many ways in which Hindus view the world and themselves in relation to faith and tradition. This chapter focuses on a few features selected from this rich history and complex worldview. Three different topics will be considered in order to look more closely at Hinduism as it is lived today.

First, Hinduism in its long history has held out a program for individual advancement. Such progress not only takes many forms and occurs over a great series of sequential rebirths, but also occurs by various means, including rituals, education, and the direct acquisition of spiritual knowledge and power within a given lifetime. As a first topic of living Hinduism a traditional set of rituals may be examined, one that extends from conception to funeral, an individual bracketing known as the **samskaras**, which highlights progressive stages in the journey of a lifebody. A survey of *samskaras* reveals one of the oldest and most enduring ritual structures of South Asia. It also illuminates important aspects of Hindu physiology, family coherence, and social structure.

Second, an entirely different sort of journey may be reviewed by considering the traditions of pilgrimages, vows, donations, and other devotional activities that occur beyond the household and, in many cases, outside the village or hometown. Again this is the realm of ritual action, as in the first topic, but this time the pan-Indian structure is far more subtle: there are no precise manuals descended from Vedic texts, no Brahman authorities hovering as essential guides, and even the definition of "ritual" at times seems stretched. The action here takes us out of house and temple to the elemental forces and rhythms of life. We could, of course, track a Hindu of either sex at these devotional tasks that with a few exceptions are not gender specific. But it seems appropriate to observe a woman engaged in her portion of what amounts to a great network of fasts, offerings, and journeys long and short because this life-support system—a lifelong devotional exercise—is primarily undertaken by the women of Hinduism. Therefore Sita's Mother is followed in a day devoted to religious duties that take her away from her family but by no means apart from its welfare. In the process of this glimpse of a few hours in the life of a woman of North India we will discover, just as with the life-cycle rites, several unifying features that assist in answering the recurrent question: What holds Hinduism together?

Third, we take up a life history, that of a forty-year-old man in South India. Whereas Sita's Mother's experiences, as related here, are typical of a North Indian woman of the twiceborn castes, Krishnayyas's life may only in some respects be called normative. His story is selected to illustrate the regional character of Hinduism noted in passing throughout these chapters. Hinduism does seem to pop up in an endless series of guises, and some of the most prominent ones carry regional tags. Here a personal history offers an opportunity to explore the area of the Godavari River delta on the Bay of Bengal coast in the Telugu-speaking state of Andhra. This subject also previews the final chapter in that this life is accomplished with one foot in traditional Hinduism and the other in modern, upwardly mobile, secular India.

Thus this chapter will consider three different sorts of passage: the life cycle, a woman's devotional routine, and a man's spiritual-academic odyssey.

The Journey of a Lifebody

> On the fourth night after the marriage and prior to first intercourse the groom addresses the bride with the verse: "May Vishnu prepare the womb, may Tvashtar mould the embryo's form, may Prajapati emit seed, may Dhatar place the embryo. Place the embryo, Sinivali, place the embryo, Sarasvati! May the Ashvins garlanded with lotuses provide the embryo, the Ahvins with their golden fire-churning sticks, the embryo that I now place for you to bear in ten months."
>
> *Jaiminiya Grihya Sutra* 1.22

Hindus recognize multiple sources of power in the world about them, sacred forces in rivers and rocks, in village temples and on hilltop shrines, even in holy women and men. It has been noted that time, like physical space, also reveals an abundance of spiritual meanings and events. There is the time of nature, a cosmic time of seasons and universal changes, measured by celestial bodies and monsoon winds, and evident in the alternations of light and darkness, warmth and cold, rain and drought, growth and decay. But there is also the time of an individual in the hoped-for span of a hundred years between birth and death. Like cosmic time, carefully segmented into memories of important events of the seasons and the deities, so too personal time is ritually marked. The marks are called *samskara*s, rites of passage and transformation.

Some ritual manuals consider as many as forty *samskara*s to be worthy of performance, but a more traditional set of ten to eighteen is characteristic. A *samskara* is literally an accomplishment, perfection, or refinement, and therefore the ritual advancement of a lifebody from its moment of conception to the moment just beyond its bodily death. Since many of the symbols are agricultural, the metaphor of ripening is often employed: a single cycle of life proceeds from seed planting to harvest sacrifice and beyond to rebirth in the succeeding cycle. Therefore food and its transformation, both material—in processes within the body—and spiritual—in ritual exchanges—remain dominant expressions.

Every culture, every religion, pays ritual attention to the life cycle. Not all of them, however, place as great an emphasis as Hinduism does upon the substantive transformations that occur in such procedures. There are several significant features of Hinduism to keep in view during a survey of the *samskara*s.

First, because of unquestioned acceptance of the concept of transmigration, the personal journey from conception to cremation or burial is not a singular one. Rather, each life is one of a great number of rebirths for that self until the achievement of its final state of liberation from the birth-and-death cycle.

Second, this personal journey of a lifebody is not a lonely one. It begins, obviously, as an extension of an existing parental family with all of its remembered forebears. It ends, ideally, with a living son, one further extension of the lineage, acting as performer of the last rites, the final sacrifice of the used-up body. If our own cultural image of the family tree is a great spreading oak or chestnut with many branches, the Hindu image is a slender bamboo, tall and undeviating, with regularly spaced joints (*vamsa,* "lineage") to represent an unbroken descent from father to son. The masculine character of this lineage is one of the central features of Hindu ritual and kinship: every attention is given to producing a son to keep the lineage and its ritual structure intact. A daughter is only a temporary member of the family, since she will be assumed into her husband's lineage, first during the marriage ceremony itself, and then, after her life in *his* village or town, again at death when she may join the company of his ancestors. From the point of view of the personal journey of each lifebody, however, it is important to remember this wider community that is involved in every ritual. It is composed not only of all the visible relatives, but the invisible ones as well. The participant presence of the deceased, both male and female, is never forgotten, and offerings of food with accompanying *mantra*s are invariably shared with them, as with the living.

Third, there is in the series of *samskara*s, to borrow a current media expression, an apparent front-loading. The majority of the rites occur before the age of six months and, in fact, several are accomplished before the severance of the umbilical cord. Since a dominant concern of the *samskara*s throughout a lifetime is refinement, that is to say, the elimination of impurities, attention is drawn once more to the previous career of this self, including its dangerous passage from body to body. What follows is the orderly sequence of *samskara*s, the ritual passage from conception through childhood, initiation, marriage, death, and beyond.

From Conception Through Childhood

Vedic manuals for domestic rituals begin the life cycle with marriage procedures. It is on the fourth night of the wedding ceremony that consummation should occur, and sexual union is actually the rite of impregnation. According to the *mantra*s of a famous wedding hymn in the *Atharvaveda,* the bride is earth and the groom is heaven. This notion of woman as cropfield and man as provider of seed remains throughout Hindu myth and experience. Furthermore, the embryo that grows in the bride as a consequence of the marriage rite is itself a new being composed partly of the father's semen—the source of bones, teeth, bodily channels, and semen—and partly of the mother's uterine blood—the source of blood, flesh, and internal organs. If the father's contributing substance predominates, the new being will be male; if the mother's is stronger, then female.

The next *samskara,* however, performed in the third month of a woman's first pregnancy, is the "generation of a male." This indicates that ritual action may still determine the sex of the fetus. Beans, barley, berries, or banyan tree shoots may all play a part in the ritual. In the fourth or a later month is the ritual "parting of the hair" in which the father-to-be parts his wife's hair three times upward, from front to back, using for a "comb" a porcupine quill, tufts of sacred grass, or a full spindle. Ripening fruits are also employed in this ceremony that, like the others, takes place at the hearth fire of the home and involves special *mantra*s. In some parts of India the mother-to-be looks at cooked rice, envisioning the child yet to be born.

The ritual of birth itself is performed immediately upon delivery, before the umbilical cord is severed. The first part of this *samskara* concentrates on the "production of wisdom" in the newborn; the father touches the baby's lips with a gold spoon or ring dipped in honey, curds, and clarified butter. *Vak* (sacred "Speech") is whispered three times into the infant's right ear. The second part of the rite includes *mantra*s for "long life." After the cutting of the cord the infant may be given a secret name, known only to the mother and father, before being installed at the mother's breast.

In the Vedic period several mysterious feminine powers were in attendance during birth, functioning as midwives of the child's destiny as well as its physical arrival into the world. Worship of the Goddess Shasthi ("Sixth") on the sixth day of life is a contemporary survival of such ancient feminine guardian figures.

Ten or twelve days after delivery (or in some areas, one year later), the baby undergoes the name-giving *samskara* and receives an everyday name, often that of an astrologically appropriate deity, by which she or he will be known. This name serves as a "cover" or distraction from the real one, still a secret from the evil eye or other dangerous element. Amulets, black threads around the wrist, lampblack marks on the body, and other devices may also guard the child from now until puberty or later.

Some time in the fourth month the newest addition to the family may be taken out of the house for the first time. That event, witnessing the sun and the moon, is a *samskara*, as is the moment of first feeding with solid food (cooked rice), usually in the sixth month. A month or so later is the ear-piercing ceremony, the earlobes being ringed with wire, the right ear first for boys, the left one first for a girl. Ritual shaving of the head and direct removal of impurities held by the hair is an important procedure throughout life in Hinduism and is often connected with special pilgrimages and vows as well as standard rites of passage. Thus the first such tonsure is the forerunner of a continuing voluntary ritual. When the hair is shaved away a small lock is left at the back of the bare skull, a twist of hair as a visible reminder of this consecration. Incidentally, the first tonsure rite is the only *samskara* that may be performed in a temple, often an ancestral goddess temple, as well as in the home. A secondary tonsure for males in their sixteenth year is sometimes considered a *samskara,* this one including the first shaving of facial hair as well as the scalp.

Education, Marriage, and Adulthood

The most powerful of *samskaras* between birth and marriage is certainly the initiatory thread-ceremony known as the **upanayana**, the ritual "leading near" of a student to his *guru* for religious instruction. Nowadays only the most exacting Brahman families request such a performance for a son; more frequently an abbreviated version serves as a preliminary to the marriage vows.

Through the Vedic era and on into classical Hinduism the *upanayana* was the indispensable second birth for all twiceborn classes, that is, the Brahmans, Kshatriyas, and Vaishyas, who received their threads at the ages of eight, eleven, and twelve, respectively. Being "born again," bound for lifetime by a sacred thread worn over the left shoulder, was a transition of great community as well as personal significance. An initiate was not merely introduced to the Vedic tradition, both textual and sacrificial, when he heard from his *guru* the first *mantra* (the **gayatri**, which is *Rigveda* 3.62.10) and learned from him the procedures for offering into the sacrificial fire (the standard **homa**). At that moment he became a link in the ageless transmission of knowledge and assumed his part of human responsibility for maintaining cosmic truth and order. No small step was that.

The elaborate ritual itself opened the door to the first stage of life, that of the student "living according to *brahman,*" the *brahmacarin,* receptive to his *guru* and all that this spiritual father would turn over to him in this lengthy birthing process. The *Atharvaveda* speaks with awe of the Vedic student more powerful than a thousand suns. Still today a few Brahman boys from special families follow the ancient tradition, living in the home of the *guru* for a period of years, learning daily the Vedic texts, orally, one line at a time, reciting the line back until the entire Veda, or significant parts of several Vedas, are committed to memory.

Another *samskara* marked the other end of the *brahmacarin's* career, the "return" to the parental home after a ritual bath signifying graduation. The second stage of life, that of the married householder, became the focus of ritual attention. The ancient stu-

A twelve-year-old Brahman boy in a North Indian village undergoing initiation (upanayana) *into sacred* mantras *and offerings on the day before his marriage. He is instructed here in the art of writing. The day-long ritual proceeds facing the ritual fire and a sacred tree with a large decorated pot representing the goddess. The boy wears an antelope skin and holds his sacred staff, symbol of the Vedic student. On this day he receives the sacred thread that he will always wear over his left shoulder.*

dent received his entire education during the years with his teacher; nowadays, of course, a Brahman boy will normally be in public schools like everyone else. Today the tradition has been trimmed down to a symbolic studenthood of the religious life: the investiture with the thread, whispering of the Gayatri *mantra,* instructions in domestic sacrifice, and the ritual bath and "return" all occur on the same day in the boy's own home, usually on the day before his departure for the marriage ceremony that takes place in the village or town of the bride.

The marriage arrangements, for all castes, are the responsibilities of parents, and preparations may take a great many months. The ceremony proper, a *samskara* transforming both bride and groom, occurs at night in the house of the bride's father. It is embedded in a wide range of other rituals and local practices that may go on for several days and usually have all the traits of a community festival. One preliminary ritual of significance, done in the privacy of the respective bride's and groom's homes well in advance, is the anointing of their bodies with an oil of turmeric, the yellow root known for its powers of fertility.

Already in the ancient period there were many variations of procedures and levels of symbolism in this union of two individuals, two cosmic principles, male and female. Modern India has even greater diversity in this universally observed *samskara,* but a number of features have carried over from the Vedic manuals and may be recognized in most parts of India and the wider Hindu world today. These include construction of a ritual booth of auspicious banana and mango leaves, tying of a thread around the wrist of the bride, first gazing of the couple at one another after the removal of a separating cloth, placing the bride's foot three times on the family grinding stone as a vow of fidelity, the important seven steps northward from or around the ritual fire, an initial offering into the hearth of the new home. The *homa* that the boy learned in his initiation is now performed with the bride as the pair assumes the role of householders in the community. Together they observe the pole star, Dhruva, and the nearby star, Arundhati (wife of the sage Vasistha), who is, like Dhruva, a model of loyalty and steadfastness. Usually there is a ritual marking of the part in the bride's hair with a stroke of vermilion, a signal to all of her marital status but also the symbol and promise of her powerful new role as mother-to-be.

Death and Beyond

The last *samskara* in the journey of a lifebody is the ritual disposal of the material body after death, either by cremation or by burial. This is a "final offering," as the *samskara* is named. Cremation and burial are both known from the time of the *Rigveda,* and both are widely practiced in Hinduism today (although the tendency for higher caste groups is to burn, for lower caste groups in South India to bury the dead). Funerary rites highlight once again Hinduism's claim that death is a continuing experience in the long course toward liberation, while the self in process remains indestructible.

This *samskara* declares the same ends as all the previous ones. It celebrates the completion of a stage of life, in this case, the end of the lifebody. It refines, by eliminating impurities and rendering the entire material body into ashes or earth. And it promotes, by liberating the subtle body for another birth in the long course. Again, this set of rituals, like the preceding ones, is subject to wide variation, but the traditional ritual sequence includes preparation of the body in or just outside the home; a procession to the burning-ground or cemetery, both usually found together at a river bank in or just outside the village or town; a ritual lighting of the pyre or placing of the body in the grave; circumambulation of the pyre or grave by the chief mourner, usually the eldest living son, who is the "offerer" of his father's body; the breaking of a large ceramic pot of water over the fire or grave; ritual bathing by the mourners along with shaving and tonsure of the men; the symbolic or actual gifting of a cow. If cremation is the means of disposal, a bone-gathering ceremony follows; later these fragments are dispersed in a sacred river.

More or less elaborate preparations, depending upon the ritual and financial status of the mourners, are immediately begun to promote the deceased on to a new journey. No longer technically *samskaras*, these **shraddhas**, as they are called, constitute a whole ritual enterprise in itself and an important dimension of Hindu life and thought, as already noted in chapter four.

To summarize and reflect upon what can be learned from this review of a life cycle according to Hinduism, a number of insights into the tradition as a whole become available. For example, there are correspondences between cosmic time and personal time, as well as an apparent symmetry of generation and regeneration. The seed of a lifebody is ritually placed in the field-womb, where it germinates after ten lunar months ("days"). After death the used-up body is ritually devoured by the funeral fire or the earth and a new temporary body is ritually begun, one that also germinates after ten days, then functions to carry the self to the company of ancestors. The clustering of essential rituals at the points of birth and death-rebirth is best understood in this light.

Throughout these rituals there are strong continuities with the oldest layers of Hinduism. It is perhaps in the *samskaras* and ancestor rites that India best remembers its ancient Vedic heritage. Basic *samskaras* have endured through centuries of changes in doctrine and practice. They proved to be an all-Indian template, a unifying pattern that countered the regional diversities and popular innovations that inevitably sprang up across the subcontinent. Of course not every householder today performs the entire set of *samskaras*, but everyone knows the system, participates in the most essential ones, and attempts, even if the scale is abbreviated or several rites are telescoped into a single performance, to accomplish as many as possible on the oldest surviving male child. Here, too, we learn of the ritual need for a continuing lineage, a link in the living present to connect the ancestors to those not yet born, a link who must by long tradition be male provider of seed. And as noted more than once, in these rituals there is an underlying spiritual basis for Hindu physiology.

Above all, a lifebody does not begin, nor does it remain, whole, pure, or safe. It requires ritual prescriptions in a lifelong process of ripening and refinement. This process is accomplished within the context of the family and its sacred hearth. Household deities may be invoked or mentioned, but no one of them is credited with these mysterious transformations. The male head of the household or an invited Brahman priest is the outward visible performer, but it is the ritual "work" itself that succeeds in refining, shaping, perfecting the ongoing lifebody and advancing it on yet another step on the path toward ultimate liberation.

Beyond the Household: A Woman's Devotions

A small town incorporates the ruins of a twelfth-century fort. Pilgrims passing from a regional temple to the train station are led aside by a local self-appointed guide, who halts the troop before a gaping hole, a partially collapsed tunnel at the base of the fort, and tells them grandly that if they dare to enter, and persevere, they will eventually emerge in Kashi. The troop gazes at the hole appreciatively and that is sufficient. One of them presents a coin to the guide and all of them turn toward the railway and the next temple town, reassured that Kashi, the holy city of Banaras, a thousand miles off by rail, is really just the other side of the hole they have now witnessed.

Rajahmundry, October 1980

There is a marvelous way in which Hinduism—and India—shake down space and time into absorbable bits. Not far from the fort in the preceding passage, in an isolated hamlet curled about a broad circular pond, villagers will tell you of the most remarkable event within memory: "Not so very long ago" an elderly villager, now deceased, rose earlier than usual and went to the pond to bathe. There in the predawn mist he discovered the famed seven *rishi*s engaged in their morning ablutions, the very sages who long ago at the dawn of time first heard the Vedas.

Duplicates or complements of these examples could be collected from virtually any region of India. The vivid spiritual imagination of Hinduism naturally and consistently fashions links to places and periods enriched by formative events (in these samples, the powerful locus of Kashi, where the *rishi*s lived, and the time when the Vedas were apprehended and made available to humankind). Established by links to these great events, and the recounting of them, local time and space are therefore resonant with their sacred force. The village, river, hilltop, anthill is not in isolation but directly connected to cosmic models of ultimate authority.

But interestingly, at the same time that each puzzle piece stresses its continuities with the grand subcontinental picture, each local element is also quick to promote its uniqueness, its Hinduism-found-nowhere-elseness. It is not surprising, of course, to note innumerable special claims to authority in the vastness of Hindu mythology, legend, and ritualism. What is remarkable is the modest self-image of each of these special claims that allows it to be just a piece in the overall design and not a whole puzzle among many other puzzles. How does that work?

For example, the preceding chapters have shown that Hinduism values the Goddess under an extraordinary range of local names (as if all the female saints of Christianity from Brigid to Teresa were to be seen as manifestations of a single feminine power). Illustrating this theme of unity and diversity is one well-known myth of the dismemberment of the goddess Sati, wife of Shiva, by the discus-weapon of Vishnu. Shiva, grief-stricken over the fiery suicide of Sati, abandoned his celestial duties and flew wildly about in the heavens with her body over his shoulder. To restore him to normalcy Vishnu hurled his discus skyward. Each time the discus struck the lifeless body a piece of Sati fell to earth, until finally more than fifty portions of the self-sacrificing Goddess descended. From the oneness of Goddess Sati came multiple parts that returned to the oneness of Goddess Earth. Today Hindu pilgrims proceed with reverence into temples and shrines that incorporate each unique fragment—the left little finger, the genitals, the tongue, the right breast—as if the pilgrimage map of India were an interstate highway of relics. India itself is in this way the immortal Goddess. But the pilgrim devotee, while affirming the unity of the Goddess tradition, pays particular attention to each site, with its special claim and its own story to relate.

With this remarkable notion of unity and plurality in mind a second topic may be examined for some of the themes of devotion that occur outside home and family. Although less formal than the routines of worship in temples and home shrines, the activities of vows, fasts, pilgrimages, and local shrines are among the oldest and most significant of Hinduism. Unlike the *samskaras*, they have little or no basis in Vedic religion, and yet their roles are so integral within Hinduism that they seem always to have been its basic territory.

These rites may be examined by following a woman who lives in a cluster of villages in eastern Uttar Pradesh, a Hindi-speaking state of North India. Since the birth of her first child, Sita (a daughter named after the heroine-goddess of the *Ramayana*), she has been called by her husband and relatives Sita's Mother. A day on which to observe her and listen to her thoughts is selected, the first day of the bright half of Jyestha and also a Sunday.

Sita's Mother disentangled herself from the grasp of her four-year-old son, rose from the rope-bed in the courtyard of her house, made her way through the mud-walled lanes by starlight to the field to relieve herself, then quickly departed for the river. She bathed rapidly in her sari, then composed herself standing waist-deep in water, enveloped in mist. Of all the moments in the day this was the finest: she was alone with the dark cleansing purity of the river, cool before the sun burned off the mist, filled with love and gratitude for Being. She raised her hands—palms together, fingers widespread, thumbs to her bowed forehead—and recited her morning prayers with her eyes closed.

On the bank she wrapped herself in a clean sari and slipped out of the wet one. She emptied from a corner knot of her sari a handful of rice grains onto the spread cloth of a *sadhu* who sat in silence on the top step of the riverbank. Other bathers were approaching as she took the familiar path home; it was too dark to recognize faces, but one acknowledged her in passing with "Jai Ram" and the blessing of Lord Rama, and she knew the voice. She carried a small brass pot of river water in her right hand, and halfway home she circled a banyan tree three times, then poured half the water at the roots where a slab of stone carved with twined serpents was leaning. Someone had already lighted a tiny mustard-oil lamp on the stone. Two more stops were also routine, one to touch the raised mace of a crude stone statue of Hanuman splashed with vermilion paint, the other to acknowledge the whitewashed square of stones that represented the Dih Baba, the guardian deity on watch here midway between the hamlets of the village cluster. For all three—the banyan and serpent tree, Hanuman, and the Dih Baba—she had special verses in the Bhojpuri dialect of Hindi she had learned as a child. Crossing the threshold of the house she recited another couplet, this one in Sanskrit, a *mantra* taught to her by her husband invoking the god Shiva, the goddess Gauri, and other deities. Then she touched the little image of Ganesha on the kitchen shelf, started the hearth-fire with a prayer, and set the rice to boil. Daughters Sita and Priya were waked and prompted to their task of creating auspicious rice-flour designs on the ground outside the front door. By now it was 4:30, and her husband had returned from his river bath. She followed his sonorous prayers from the other room and knew, as from a clock on the wall, the time remaining before her departure.

Entrusting the serving of food to the girls, and allowing her youngest to sleep until dawn, she was packed and on the path toward the crossroad bus stop, exhilarated, despite a forty-eight-hour fast, excited as she focused on her journey. By sunup the bus arrived and lurched off toward the nearby town and its railway station. The train was an hour or so behind schedule. As she sat on the platform a small, whiskered man with large, liquid eyes came and stood silently before her. Sita's Mother bent over her belongings and unpacked the nested set of steel containers she had brought from home. The old man's companion, a young, nearly naked fellow with one arm missing at the shoulder, joined him, and the pair squatted before their benefactress, tin bowls gradually filling with scooped handfuls. A little girl of five expanded the pair to a trio and the one-armed man began to empty his bowl into her bucket. The hot rice moved from tiffin to bowl to bucket under appreciative smiles. All retired in different directions, the child to divide her blessing with her mother, the men to sit and be joined by other men who silently spread dirty cloths on the platform to receive a share of a share. All ate rapidly, then washed bowls, hands, and mouths at the railway water faucet, elbow to elbow with Sita's Mother who was scouring the empty tiffin set. Two scruffy dogs went after the remnants in the drain as their portion of the feast. Not a word was spoken throughout the ceremony.

By the time she descended from the train at her stop it was nearly noon, and Sita's Mother faced a strenuous walk in dreadful heat. From the experience of previous pilgrimage fasts she knew how to conserve strength, not just for getting there, but also for the endless return journey to a ritual bath in the river before food. This pilgrimage was a first for her, one long planned as she learned its details from other women in the village. Unlike a pilgrimage to a famous temple or a celebrated river during its festival season, her goal this time was a tree. It was, in fact, another banyan tree, just like the one at home by the river. But this one was unique: it was regarded locally as the very tree under which a man was restored to life, not by his own merit, not by the grace of Vishnu, Shiva, or

A line of women pilgrims walking barefoot along the Ganges River in a five-day, fifty-mile circumambulation of Kashi (Banaras). They carry food, bedding, and a supply of small coins and grains to toss to beggars and ascetics as well as to offer to the deities of 108 shrines and temples along the path.

Durga, but by the quick-wittedness and persistent devotion of his wife. Sita's Mother told the story to her children every year at this time when she performed, usually at the banyan tree by the river, the Vow of Savitri.

> One day long ago the king's son, Satyavat, was collecting wood in the forest when he collapsed beside a great banyan tree. Yama, Death, appeared with his terrible noose to carry off another soul. But Satyavat's wife, Savitri, came just in time and pursued them. Yama repeatedly insisted that she go home and let him do his godly work. With each remonstrance Savitri became even more determined, impressing Yama so deeply with her eloquent loyalty to her husband that at last he granted her a series of three wishes. For the third wish Savitri requested many sons, forcing the hand of Death to relinquish Satyavat and allow him to father sons with this faithful and resolute woman. Satyavat came to under the banyan tree, remembering nothing of this ordeal, and together they returned to the village where eventually they raised many fine sons.

Now Sita's Mother could see this renowned tree and at last she entered its canopy of shade, a vast space of incredibly cooling relief from the 120-degree plain. More than a hundred people, mostly women, were within its multitrunked shade, but altogether they filled only part of this living arena. It was the largest tree she had ever seen, and as magnificent as any temple. After a brief rest she deposited a coin on the shrine set up by a self-appointed priest, then took a large spool of cotton thread from her bag and began to circle the central trunk, slowly adding her white thread to hundreds of others. With the tree always on her right, she prayerfully wound her thread the sacred number of times, 108, and for the hour that it required kept in mind, as she had been instructed, the health, prosperity, and longevity of her husband, her desire for a second, perhaps even a third son, and a plea for herself to avoid widowhood.

In tracking Sita's Mother for this portion of a day we observe something of the diversity and surprising subtlety of Hindu ritual life. Both the tenor of women's rituals and the importance of minor details of ritual performance are deserving of comment here. First, the significance of rituals performed by women in Hinduism cannot be overestimated. Although largely unrepresented in published manuals in Sanskrit, underrepresented in the more available ritual booklets in regional languages, and not generally discussed by the male priests of village or urban institutions (shrines, temples, *mathas*, monasteries), women's religious activities are nevertheless understood to be the cement that holds together Hindu society at its basic level, the family. Like married women throughout the Hindu world, Sita's Mother accomplished the Vow of Savitri in accord with a version of this popular tale. It is found in one of the epics (the *Mahabharata*), several of the Puranas, and illustrated devotional tracts in every language of India. Her renewal of her marriage vow to be a steadfastly loyal wife was no mere statement of conjugal duty; it was, and continues to be, in the annual performance of this vow and many others of a similar character, a recognition of her sacred obligation and role of protectress of her family. The Savitri Vow and certain others are directly concerned with the physical and spiritual well-being of males—husbands, sons, brothers. They are accomplished entirely without them. And they can be performed only by an auspicious woman, one whose great powers of fertility, prosperity, wealth, abundance, long life (all the powers, that is, of the goddess herself) are properly directed to continue the patriarchal lineage. In other words, her powers must be properly channeled by traditional marriage.

Sita's Mother displays the marks of such an auspicious woman: the vermilion mark in the part of her hair, first placed there by her husband as the binding act in the marriage ritual; a spot of color on her forehead; bangles on her arms; rings on her toes; red paint on her bare feet. Her prayers while circling the banyan tree included a plea to avoid becoming a widow. In traditional India the condition of a widow is proverbially labeled a "fate worse than death." It is a painful deprivation not only of the colorful, opulent display of the above symbols of auspiciousness, but even of basic physical needs and liberties. However, the main reason for such a plea to Savitri is that widowhood is a direct signal of failure to protect a husband. Some lapse in her devotion, chastity, or dutiful performance can allow fate to take his life before hers. A widow must live with a dual reproach as one who failed her husband and one for whom the marriage ritual no longer directs her considerable powers into safe and benevolent rewards. However, for the family of Sita's Mother all is well, even as it was for the family of Savitri, and credit for present well-being is as clear as it was in the model of long ago.

The focus has been on a particular type of women's rites in Hinduism, a minor pilgrimage, a one-person journey by a family protectress. A pilgrimage, even a short one to a regional site with its local myths, legends, and procedures, is a fairly obvious example of religious observance. It has a journey to and a journey from the sacred site framing the actions performed there. But there are many other details of ritual in the day of a Hindu woman or man that might escape the outsider's attention were it not for verbal and nonverbal clues, the grace, reverence, even affection that attend such everyday actions (*karma*s) as entering or crossing a river, watering a plant or tree, preparing food.

For example, handouts to beggars might easily be dismissed as an occasional response to the circumstances of poverty, but such a view loses sight of several definitive aspects of Hinduism. Giving, *dana,* whether a wealthy patron's gift of a new temple to his town or the casual tossing of food remnants to ants, ghosts, or "beings" in the most generic and anonymous of senses, is ritual activity. Of the five prescribed daily "sacrifices" all involve reverent giving to other beings, and one in particular is directed to other humans in acts of hospitality or donation. Also, in sacrifice or giving, whatever the scale and duration, the sacrificer or the giver is altered, the merit of the event being added on to the lifebody of the sacrificer.

In this sense, the incidental beggars on the railway platform were just one more group in the large, amorphous company of ritual recipients of Sita's Mother's activities on this day, as she herself, consciously or unconsciously in the ritual routine, was the recipient of merit and spiritual advancement. And such merit as she obtained was of course extended to her family, whose nourishment was her constant selfless duty. The beggars blended in with the *sadhu* on the riverbank, the would-be priest at the famed tree, the village deities, the household gods who first received the food she prepared in the predawn darkness, and indeed the trees at home at the sacred site and the Ganges River into which she had prayerfully tossed a coin as the train rattled over the long railway bridge.

A Region, a River, and a Life

> One dew-wet morn, here, I unfolded my life, and practiced my songs on a harp. This harp of my life's entirety I know I must leave behind—but their airs, filling my heart, I shall take with me.
>
> Rabindranath Tagore (1861–1941)[9]

The past forty years have witnessed changes in India that rival those of the previous forty centuries. For example, the rapid spread of television in the 1980s brought the immediacy and concrete, specific awareness so characteristic of video imagery to many remote areas of the subcontinent. More available than the automobile, more personal than radio, more versatile than the fantasy-world cinema, a single TV set in a village suddenly opens that small society to alternate realities and presents to its people entirely new options. Life in the smallest village in Kerala is linked visually, and thereby realistically, to life in Bombay and Delhi, or to rural Assam or Madhya Pradesh.

Individuals in the complex of Indian civilization have experienced twentieth-century changes in different ways and to varying

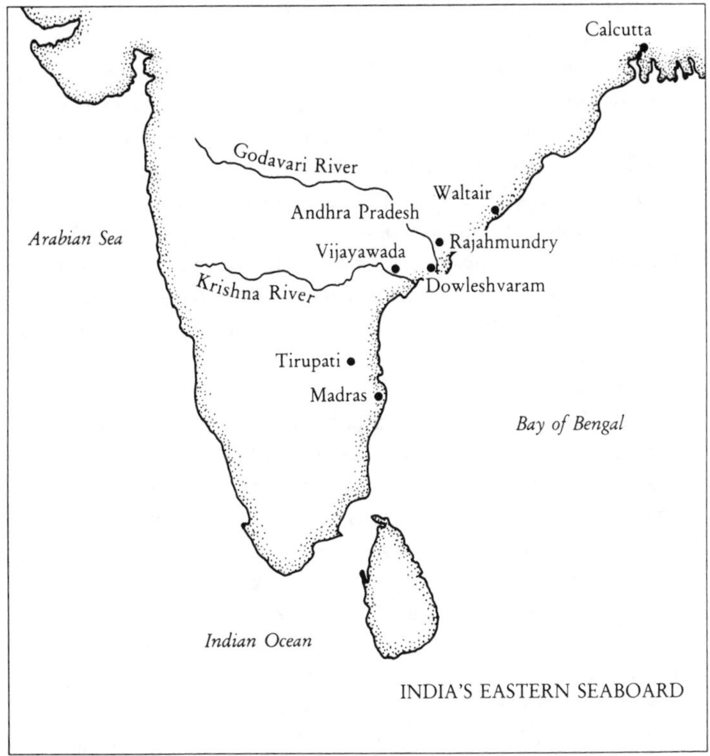

INDIA'S EASTERN SEABOARD

degrees; most have had to adapt to new economic, political, social, and religious realities, and many have had to devise a more or less fluid stance between the poles of traditional and posttraditional life-styles. A closer look at one individual may instruct about certain aspects of Hinduism today. It would be impossible to find in so diverse and multicultural a subcontinent as India a "typical" Hindu. In some ways the life history we are about to survey is atypical, particularly in the last two decades. But his roots are traditional, and characteristic of his region, and his experiences are not at all remote from those of his countrymen in other regions. He is selected for this chapter because he is open, reflective, and articulate about his life and also because his life as a whole represents a composite—familiar throughout the long history of Hinduism—of several modes of being a Hindu.

M. V. Krishnayya (his real name, used with his approval following interviews 1980–1987) has lived all but a year of his life on the southeastern coast of India in the Telugu-speaking state of Andhra Pradesh. He was born in 1946 in the village of Dowleshvaram on the left bank of one of India's greatest rivers, the nine-hundred-mile-long Godavari. His family belongs to the Golla or Shepherd caste of the Shudra *varna;* in the ordering of castes in the region Gollas are in the median ranks. As is the case with many castes with occupational names, Gollas in contemporary India are involved in a wide variety of trades and professions outside the traditional one.

Dominating Krishnayya's childhood memory is the vast expanse of the river, considered auspicious at Dowleshvaram where a forty-mile-long delta begins. Morning baths, riverside ceremonies, immersion of household and festival images, all link human and riverine cycles as the Godavari changes from monsoon ferocity to dry season docility. Overlooking the river from a Dowleshvaram hilltop is a temple of Vishnu (who is here called Janardhana) with its great carved wooden festival cart housed in a shed just across the street from Krishnayya's house. And down the street, almost at the center of the village, is the temple of Shiva.

On the outskirts, where the crop fields begin, are half a dozen small shrines of disease goddesses, but closer to Krishnayya's street are two more substantial goddess centers, one a temple of Ankalamma, the other a shrine for Mutyalamma, both of them recipients of chickens sacrificed at their altars. Mutyalamma is the village guardian deity and Sister to everyone in Dowleshvaram. Her shrine on its square base includes a Nim tree and numerous stones. Krishnayya remembers his parents saying, "Mutyalamma is not in the shrine, so we [the village] are going to bring her here from her mother-in-law's place." In Mutyalamma's honor, each house has a fresh yellow turmeric patch on one interior wall, with three dots and two stripes representing the goddess. And an earthen pot containing water from the daily washing of rice is allowed to ferment slowly; in Krishnayya's house it is kept by his mother on a bed of leaves; it represents Mutyalamma's presence in the house, providing health, well-being, and coolness. It was quite a different presence, Krishnayya recalls, from that of the little images of Lakshmi and Krishna that were worshiped in the household shrine. The local Washerman, shrine priest for both Mutyalamma and Ankalamma, became possessed by one or the other goddess whenever she needed to express her anger to the villagers. Krishnayya remembers a terrible smallpox epidemic when he was ten or eleven; hundreds died, including someone from nearly every household.

"According to my parents," says Krishnayya, "we are Vaishnavas, in the tradition of Ramanuja. But we went more often to the Shiva temple, and our family priest was a Shaiva." More influential upon Krishnayya in his early years than temple traditions were the many rituals performed by his mother. Krishnayya was the fourth child born in the family, but the first to survive, and he remained exceptionally close to his mother. He remembers circling with her the "Tulsi Fort," a basil plant sacred to Vishnu, while she performed her daily *puja* with a lamp of oil. Among the many women's rituals called *nomu*s in Telugu he particularly recalls one in which he accompanied his mother in house-to-house distribution of green grams, soaked in water, to all the village. "Don't you want to have a sister?" he was asked repeatedly, for the ceremony, his mother's vow, was to gain another child.

Krishnayya also remembers absorbing "what everybody knows," for example, about the many objects hung from doorways, gates, and rooftops to ward off the evil eye or about the *mantra*s recited, especially to Anjaneya (Hanuman), to frighten demons while walking at noon and midnight or about all the things that are auspicious or inauspicious for first "sight" at the start of the day or any important undertaking.

Krishnayya has seen a photo taken on the day when, at six months, his ears were ritually pierced and ringed. But the first of the *samskara*s that he remembers was his initial tonsure at the age of five years, on a memorable day for him when the family journeyed over the immense Godavari River to the temple of Lord Venkateshvara in "little Tirupati." There Krishnayya had his head shaved while his eleven-month-old brother underwent the *samskara* of first feeding with solid food. Back in Dowleshvaram the ceremonies were repeated by the family priest and then, shortly after, came the ritual that began Krishnayya's formal education.

The schoolteacher and the family priest both came to the house, and Krishnayya observed closely as the priest wrote a prayer to Shiva in rice grains spread on a great brass tray. Verses to Sarasvati, the goddess of learning, were taught and then a new slate received *puja*s, and on it were written first "OM" and then the letters of the Telugu alphabet, beginning with "A." Krishnayya made the ritual presentation of gifts to the priest and the teacher, as well as new slates and chalk to all the students in his new class.

A significant part of Krishnayya's education took place outside home and school. A Brahman widow with shaved head lived next door, and Krishnayya spent considerable time with her. His mother would lift him over the garden wall to the widow, who called him "Gopalam" and read to him stories from the *Ramayana,* the *Mahabbharata,* and the *Bhagavata Purana.* Krishnayya was repeatedly cautioned never to touch her, as she was a Brahman. From her he learned not only the great tales of gods, demons, and heroes, but also of India's famous cities, Banaras, Calcutta, Puri. She would periodically go on pilgrimage to one of these mysterious places, then return to tell him more about *samsara, karma,* and *moksha,* about heaven and hell, and even of the Buddhist doctrine of emptiness.

Gradually, with his family increased by two brothers and two sisters, Krishnayya came to know the temples and towns of his region, and horse- or bullock-carts, busses, and trains took them all to the great festivals. After his initial tonsure Krishnayya had his head ritually shaved another dozen times in twenty years, in connection with various vows, school examinations, and diplomas. One such tonsure was in the Satya Narayana temple on the hill at Annavaram, another at the temple of Venkateshvara in greater Tirupati, India's wealthiest temple, situated far to the south in the Seven Hills. At twelve years Krishnayya traveled for the first time outside Andhra, experiencing briefly a new language, Tamil, and a bewildering urban culture in the city of Madras. The year before this his world had already begun to widen when he started his studies in both Hindi and English. Krishnayya was the first in his family to learn English. As a child he heard not only the multiple dialects of Telugu, but also Urdu, Oriya, Marathi, Tamil, Kannada, Hindi, and English, but only as he started to travel did he begin to link language with region, religion, class, and education.

Krishnayya tried also to start Sanskrit, but was removed from the roster. "It will be difficult for you," said the teacher. In other words, says Krishnayya, "I was not a Brahman."

Krishnayya's father was not able to work for a time, and the family suffered considerably. When the priest came to inform them that the third anniversary funerary observance for Krishnayya's deceased grandfather was due, and would cost ten rupees, there was no money. Krishnayya sold his books for that amount, a gesture that left him uneasy; in his twelve-year-old thoughts it was like selling the goddess Sarasvati.

After finishing high school in Dowleshvaram, Krishnayya received a modest scholarship to study in the Government Arts College in Rajahmundry, where he followed his father's wishes and pursued a science degree. He was also introduced to the ways of life in a large town. Mathematics courses he found trying, and he spent several years on the degree, with interruptions of employment as a government clerk in a forest area of central Andhra, and then for three years in the city of Vijayawada. His religious life in these years away from home was intense, with numerous *puja*s at the Shiva temple or up on the hillside at the ancient temple of Durga in Vijayawada. As part of his early morning *puja* each day he worshiped the *navagraha*s, or nine planets, including Surya, the sun; he also had special reverence for Ganesha, Sarasvati, and Lakshmi. To his mother he gave a framed lithograph of Venkateshvara, Lord of the Seven Hills, which she incorporated into the home shrine in the kitchen at Dowleshvaram. Frequently he heard religious discourses at the Ramakrishna Math in Vijayawada, and once he asked a visiting swami from Kanchipuram for his blessing in anticipation of an exam; receiving it, Krishnayya felt exhilaration that his boldness had brought him within the aura of a holy man.

When he was accepted at Andhra University to begin, at age twenty-five, a degree in philosophy, he was drawn back across the wide Godavari to Waltair, on the coast of northern Andhra. There was money for tuition only, so he slept at first outside the door of the student hostel. At times in that initial year, perhaps because of a necessary asceticism, the religious life seemed powerfully attractive to him. He began to reexamine his religious experiences and think about the "logic" of Hinduism. He was aware that he was going to temples less for *vrata*s or personal problem solving, more for aesthetic and religious enjoyment. He also reflected on what the Brahman widow had taught him about the *atman,* about the importance of self-discovery ahead of self-gratification.

His university studies in both Indian and Western philosophy led him through an M.A. degree program and appointment as a research scholar and candidate for the Ph.D. in philosophy. His close friends among foreign students at the university included Russians and Americans, and he absorbed from them ideas, attitudes, language, everything that aroused his abundant curiosity. Russian became his fourth language, and he earned an interpreter's certificate, Russian-English-Russian. A research fellowship to work in the National Library in Calcutta took him out of Andhra for a year and led not only to a fifth linguistic fluency, in Bengali, but also to a friendship with a fellow student, resulting in 1975 in the unusual step of a self-chosen marriage. The union was against outraged protests on both sides; although of the same caste, their different regions were seen by the elders as insuperable barriers. The bride's father refused to attend and perform the important giving-away ceremony, so that was done by her mother. "Bengalis think we are another race," scoffs Krishnayya, "an inferior race!"

The intensity of his research program, coupled with a degree of self-consciousness in the company of foreign friends, had gradually curtailed some of his personal religious activities, and for some years he gave up his morning devotions. But as the years stretched out and his future job prospects remained unpromising he resumed worship of the nine planets each morning and undertook, on the advice of a friend, a lengthy recitation from the Puranas, a **japa** by which the sage Markandeya overcame death. Every morning for two months in 1978 he did this at home, as there was no money for a service in the temple. But the *mantra*s had no appreciable result and, despite the arrival of a daughter to the new household, Krishnayya's worries were magnified by a marriage turned quarrelsome.

By 1980 Krishnayya's position was increasingly insecure. His degree program was stalled, he had not had a job for seven years, and he had a wife and daughter to support. His mother was convinced that the village astrologer could help, and the tall, gaunt Brahman with the musty Sanskrit manuscripts and brass zodiac dials was consulted. In the mail Krishnayya received a large packet of horoscopes: the standstill, according to the astrologer, resulted from the longtime evil influence of Saturn and Mars, two of the nine planets in Hindu astrology. After some resistance Krishnayya acceded to his mother's request that he make ritual presentations (*danas*) to a special Brahman designated by the astrologer. He took the train from Waltair to Rajahmundry, then a rickshaw (pedicab) to the village. The *puja* arranged by the family priest was brief: Krishnayya sat opposite a Brahman brought from outside the village, one of a special class willing to assume, for a fee, the misfortunes of others. Under the instructions of the family priest, Krishnayya transferred from a brass tray to this Brahman a bag of black grams, two iron nails, sesame seeds, cotton threads, and some raw sugar, along with the invisible but dangerous effects of Saturn and Mars, which the visiting Brahman would in turn remove from his own person at home by means of another ritual expiation.

Krishnayya was reluctant to credit the ritual, but he readily admitted that his fortunes showed marked improvement from that point on, as did those of his brother, who performed about the same time a similar rite to remove the unfavorable effects of Rahu

Krishnayya (left) consults a roadside fortune-teller in Rajahmundry, 1985. A parrot selects a card from the deck and gives it to the fortune-teller, who interprets its signs for the client.

and Ketu. Eventually his dissertation was completed and accepted, and Krishnayya received an appointment on the faculty of the Department of Philosophy at the university. This brought relief from painful economic worries and eased some of the tensions in the family. Krishnayya's horizons continued to expand: in 1985 he was invited abroad and traveled to London and throughout the United States, then returned to Waltair to teach and begin work on a book. As he examines his fortieth year he reflects on the constant changes that occur in a life, like those that stir the depths and surfaces of the Godavari River, although apparent all the while is the unity of the life, like the oneness of the river.

At a distance from the region of Andhra and the nation of India one may observe in the details of this life many features of contemporary Hinduism, including some of the more elusive ones. Though Krishnayya's name and family are traditionally Vaishnava, Shiva and various goddesses play an important part in their faith and practice. This kind of balance is typical of Hinduism. Belief systems are personal, subdued, flexible, and subordinated to practical expressions of faith in vows, devotions, prayers, life-cycle rituals, festivals, and pilgrimages. While these traditional family and community stepping-stones dominate, their importance fluctuates according to the period of life and specific challenges of that period.

This survey of Krishnayya's experiences, a tiny fraction of them at best, is instructive in another way. It undercuts the "classical"/"folk" dichotomy that is sometimes used to discuss Indian tradition. The Brahman widow telling stories from the Sanskrit *Ramayana* and the untouchable priest possessed by the goddess of smallpox are both vital parts of living Hinduism in a single village and are equally important components in the faith of one individual. Krishnayya, no longer a villager, never having been a "peasant," is at ease in modern India, travels frequently, and is well acquainted with contemporary innovation and change, yet he carries in his experience those and many other parts in the composite of his Hindu background. He has ventured onto paths totally unknown to his parents, but he still is shaped by his origins and, like great numbers of his countrymen and women, must nurture a lifestyle that engages simultaneously in the old world of tradition, both "folk" and "classical," and the new world of cosmopolitan, television-viewing India.

■

CHAPTER VI

Hinduism Today

On September 4, 1987, Roop Kanwar, an eighteen-year-old woman in the village of Deorala in Rajasthan, burned to death as she sat upright, enclosed in the logs of her husband's funeral pyre. The practice of *sati,* widow burning, is an ancient one in northwest India, although without sanction in any Hindu text. Condemned by nineteenth-century reformers such as Ram Mohan Roy and prohibited by ordinances beginning in 1829, it has survived in sporadic instances in the last two centuries, one of many graphic illustrations of the manner in which India and Hinduism appear to inhabit multiple time frames.

The nationwide debate generated by the Deorala *sati* is instructive for those who seek to understand the destiny of Hinduism at the close of the twentieth century. The government of India, as a modernizing secular state under constitutional law, was swift and unanimous in passing a bill providing for life imprisonment or the death sentence for abetment of *sati.* Vigorous condemnations of this cultural anachronism appeared in the press, along with denunciation of those who would glorify *sati* by citing scriptures on women's loyalty to their husbands, even to the point of self-sacrifice. But little was said about the thousands of active shrines throughout the subcontinent that commemorate *sati* events of the past. Some prominent Hindu sectarian leaders even came out in support of "voluntary *sati*" and "*sati dharma.*" One of their arguments was that the ideal of feminine loyalty demonstrated throughout Hindu mythology, folklore, ritual, and symbolism is upheld by only a few women, just as the ideal of renunciation is maintained by only a few *samnyasi*s. Still others resisted taking a stand on the issue on the grounds of freedom of religious expression guaranteed by the constitution.

A few weeks after Roop Kanwar's death, which some witnesses stated was physically enforced by her male in-laws, a poll was conducted in thirty-two towns and villages in fourteen districts of Rajasthan.[10] A majority (63.4%) of those interviewed were women. Of those interviewed, 86.6 percent knew of the *sati* cult, 80.7 percent knew of Roop Kanwar, and 63.4 percent approved of the act in her case. Only 3.65 percent of those interviewed felt that the young woman had been forced to commit *sati*. A number of respondents declared that she had become a goddess (Sati Devi).

The forceful debate on this single event, and the public opinion of Rajasthanis, remind us of the dangers of easy generalizations about contemporary Hinduism. From a corner of a high-rise apartment complex in Bombay, Kanpur, or Hyderabad there may be no temples or shrines visible, no traditional dress, festival activities, or outward evidence of caste. By contrast, at a crossroads in a traditional town or village there may be two or three temples and half a dozen shrines and statues in sight, a local goddess procession going by, a colorfully clad *sadhu* or traditional beggar making his rounds of doorways, and ample evidence of caste distinctions in dress, occupation, and behavior. But the degree of religious faith and practice, the measure of "being a Hindu," often cannot be determined by appearances. It would be a mistake to assume that modernization and Westernization, so apparent in urban India, have erased essential Hindu traditions. Personal and family patterns of worship, participation in temples, *maths*, and other religious institutions, and visits to pilgrimage sites or ancestral shrines, although often modified or abbreviated by the exigencies of urban life, go on just as they do in villages and traditional towns.

Hinduism throughout its history has had a limitless capacity for absorbing events into its symbol system, and it continues to do so in modern times. Indira Gandhi, prime minister of India until her assassination in Delhi in October 1984, is now visible in the guise of plaster busts in every village and town. Like a goddess, she is usually at crossroads, garlanded, with a fresh red dot on her forehead, and is often revered by a largely illiterate populace that recognizes in her statue a power to see, touch, borrow. It remains to be seen whether an actual Indira cult will emerge, but already the myths are in process, translating a secular political life into a new hagiography, an illustration of Hinduism's perpetual drive for self-renewal.

One indicator of vitality and experimentation in Hinduism has been described by scholars as a process of Sanskritization, whereby Brahmanic faith and practice, and Sanskrit texts, become increasingly more significant to non-Brahman strata of society. This is, of course, a process already documented in early Vedic religion, and one that is apparent in every subsequent phase of the history of Hinduism. The Brahmans, once the educated and educating elite, protected the Sanskrit language, the Vedas, and the *shastras* and limited access to the law codes, great temples, *tirthas*, and monastic institutions. In modern India they have seen their power base eroded by the secular state, upwardly mobile caste groups, and political institutions. Education is open to all. Untouchables, tribal peoples, "backward classes," and "weaker sections" are given special catch-up privileges and positions in affirmative action programs. Temples may no longer exclude Hindu untouchables, some Vedic schools and even major temples are administered by state governments, and the Vedas and Sanskrit devotional *shlokas* can be heard by all at public bathing facilities, fairs, and festivals. Radio and TV broadcasts democratize the faith. *Mantras* are recited by women and recorded on cassettes, and the epic *Ramayana* has been serialized for Sunday morning television. A Brahman recitant is not required if the Sanskrit classics are available on a personal videocassette recorder.

Along with the decline of Brahman hegemony and the increase in universal education has come a slowly increasing affluence in the middle and lower classes that enables many to enrich their spiritual lives by a variety of means: travel to sacred sites and regional fairs and festivals; adoption of new and more elaborate rituals; religious education in *mathas* and societies; donations for shrines or temples; devotional allegiance to a godman or living goddess; purchase of religious books, tracts, and posters.

As an illustration consider a middle-aged South Indian man named Raju whose caste in the Shudra *varna* places him outside the traditional three twiceborn classes and Sanskrit learning. A spiritual conversion in his late twenties and economic independence, the result of a successful blue-collar job, propelled him into prominence as the most resourceful religious personality of his neighborhood. Essentially he has two spiritual careers that now increasingly absorb his time, one visible to the community, the other private and personal.

He is a faith healer who provides sacred ash (*vibhuti*), lime juice, and *mantras* as cures for ailments such as boils, rashes, or the bites of centipedes, scorpions, or snakes. Mothers bring to him children affected by the evil eye or by malevolent winds and spirits. He also treats adult "body weakness" caused by the influence of dark planets, and he is knowledgeable about charms, amulets, gemstones, and talismans for a variety of purposes. At certain local festivals he is an ecstatic god-dancer, one who is routinely possessed by a powerful and dangerous deity. Well known as a benefactor of religious institutions, he has personally constructed goddess shrines in different parts of his city, one for example housing the pan-Indian Durga, another for a particular epidemic disease goddess. Recently he has taken up sponsorship of a local haven for wandering *sadhus*, regularly supplying them with brass bells and begging bowls, daily leaf plates, and even pampering them with cash to assure them of what he regards as a balanced diet.

The invisible side of his religious life is more astonishing. Although a Shudra, he wears a sacred thread, and his daily meditations and rituals in a fluent Sanskrit would rival the procedures of the strictest Brahman. Following his dawn bath in the river he meditates upon the *linga* he wears always around his neck—a grey agate surrounded by minute figures of Ganesha, Lakshmi, Durga, Parvati, and Sarasvati, all enclosed in a great silver egg. One of the three small rooms in the city apartment he shares with his wife and two children is entirely devoted to minishrines and altars, and here he performs *pujas* in Sanskrit for two hours, followed by another hour of meditation, all before starting the day's work. Raju diets on milk and fruits, observes celibacy (*brahmacarya*), allows his long, matted hair to grow into Shiva's locks. He describes his goal as the Upanishadic quest: knowledge of the Supreme Soul, *brahman*.

The spiritual life of this man is a good illustration of a conscious and deliberate program of Sanskritization. It is also a corrective to the outsider's tendency to separate the shaman or faith healer of non-Sanskritic "folk" religion from the high-caste Hindu Sanskritic tradition. Riding about the city on his motor scooter, his matted locks flying in the wind, Raju seems happy to include the entire range of Hindu phenomena within his own expansive embrace.

Another process in modern India might be labeled "acharyization." This is the tendency of urban, educated classes to simplify

Hinduism by reducing it to selected pronouncements of a few great teachers (**acharyas**) and divesting it of all aspects perceived to be communal, parochial or rural, divisive, and "superstitious." A standard list of *acharya*s might begin with such medieval synthesizers as Shankara and Ramanuja, then jump to one or more recent reformer such as Ram Mohan Roy, Dayananda Sarasvati, Ramakrishna and Vivekananda, or Aurobindo. A more generous list might add Gautama Buddha, Jesus Christ, Guru Nanak, and Gandhi, and those exposed to regional swamis and *guru*s who have gained national or international followings might mention Sathya Sai Baba, Ramana Maharshi, Maharishi Mahesh Yogi, or Rajnish. Note here one incongruity demonstrated in back-to-back discussions of Sanskritization and acharyization: while Raju wears on his person the images of four goddesses (along with Shiva and Ganesha) and daily worships several other goddesses, the standard lists of respectable *acharya*s are all male.

Like Sanskritization, this phenomenon centering on *acharya*s is related to the process of democratization of the faith at the expense of the Brahman elite, as well as to increased exposure to Western values, widening educational opportunities, and the expansion of modern mass communications. (As in the United States, the media hold the power to turn religious figures into national celebrities in relatively short order.) Behind an eclectic and often dogmatic acharyized Hinduism is the desire to modernize, to demonstrate that the dominant faith of India is effective and up-to-date not only for South Asians, but for humankind, a universal faith, eternal and seminal for human spirituality. It is in effect Hinduism without warts.

Acharyized Hinduism ignores or dismisses impediments to universal acceptance of the faith. In this view the pandits' distinctions between *shruti* and *smriti*, the caste hierarchy, untouchability, concerns for purity and pollution, magic and witchcraft, astrology, faith healing, "barbarisms" such as *sati*, child sacrifice, hook swinging, fire walking, or the offerings of chickens, pigs, goats, sheep, or buffalo to local goddesses, even the profusion of gods and goddesses in Puranic myths are all left behind in the program of evolution for modern Hinduism. Emphasis is upon self-realization after the example of the self-realized teacher. The program is usually strongly egalitarian and devotional-meditative, moralizing, with emphasis on overt monotheism or the Upanishadic, Vedantic identification of the self with the divine world Soul. Frequently there is a focus on "modern scientific principles" harnessed not for pleasure and material gain (as in "the decadent West"), but for those spiritual ends manifest in the eternal *dharma* and represented by the *acharya*s.

Seldom apparent in village India and still rare in traditional towns, acharyized Hinduism is familiar in English-speaking urban sectors throughout India and has had considerable success as an export to the West, from the Theosophical Society and Ramakrishna Mission to the more recent Transcendental Meditation movement and Divine Light Mission. It is worth remarking that alongside the *guru*-establishments purveying *yoga* and hybrid, up-dated Hinduism to the West, Hindu temples and *matha*s have been steadily appearing all over Europe and America. They are built by traditional Indian masons and sculptors, dedicated and staffed by Hindu *pujari*s and pandits, and serve the large immigrant communities who now establish roots in major cities of the West. Westerners fortunate enough to visit these new institutions are treated to authentic Hindu rituals and discourses previously not seen outside India, although here too the general tendency is to foster a faith acceptable morally and intellectually to Western societies and to Hindus who have chosen to live in them.

For the vast majority of Hindus in South Asia the adjective "modern" before Hinduism holds no particular meaning. Even dynamic new movements—striking to long-time observers of South Asian religions—are perceived by the faithful as age-old, normative expressions. The sudden appearance of a popular goddess such as Santoshi Mata or the huge increase in pilgrim attention to the goddess Vaishno Devi in northwest India are phenomena readily absorbed into the patterns of classical Hindu goddess traditions. And when hundreds of thousands of black-clad, exuberant young men mobilize all over India in the burgeoning cult of Ayyappan and travel by chartered trains and busses, then on foot up Kerala's Sabari Hill to his shrine, they are after all traditional pilgrims displaying a standard repertoire of vows, devotional fervor, fasting, celibacy, and recitation of the divine name. In fact, the curious result of the endless experimentation of Hindu tradition is that true innovation is virtually impossible: it seems that in one or another age everything has already been done many times over!

Devotees from different castes, drawn together in the cult of the bachelor god Ayyappan, son of Shiva and Mohini, a feminine incarnation of Vishnu. These young men undergo a forty-one day penance and five hundred–mile pilgrimage every year.

As the world moves into the twenty-first century and India overtakes China as the most populous nation on earth, South Asia faces more pressing challenges than at any previous point in history. South Asia is riddled with communal violence—Hindu-Muslim, Sikh-Hindu, Tamil Hindu–Sinhalese Buddhist, tribal-nationalist. Despite the "green revolution" of the 1970s, oppressive poverty and malnutrition burden half the population with no relief in view. Two-thirds of the people are illiterate, and the democratic institutions of India and Sri Lanka, plus the liberal Hindu kingdom of Nepal, sandwiched between the changing regimes of neighboring nations, seem always to be targets for anarchy. But Hinduism as a dominant faith in the region of South Asia exhibits little concern for the turn of a century, of an economy, of a dynasty. Its age-old ways of listening, mythologizing, classifying, recycling, and swallowing the universe look at the world and its ills with a relative eye. This is, after all, the Kali *yuga*, the worst time, and one to be succeeded by a long rest. Then a perfected age will dawn, truth and *dharma* will be restored to fullness and plenitude, and the universal order will prevail once again—for a time.

Epilogue

On the wall beside my desk is a photo taken many years ago of a darkly gnarled tree. From its branches hang half a dozen heavy burlap packages, blackened with mildew from the rains. Together they are an awesome, mysterious image. They provide no clue as to what they are, although one suspects they may either be offerings to some local deity, ancestor, or power—named or nameless to the one who took the trouble to place them there—or bundles to draw away attention of the evil eye and therefore protect the area. As for the photo, it hangs here as a reminder of how much of Hinduism I do not understand.

Notes

1. See Bruce Lincoln, *Myth, Cosmos and Society. Indo-European Themes of Creation and Destruction* (Cambridge, Mass.: Harvard University Press, 1986), chs. 1, 2, 6.
2. The English word "caste" comes from the Portuguese *casta,* a word the sixteenth-century explorers used to render the local Indian word *jati.*
3. Trans. from Sanskrit by Chakravarti Rajagopalachari, *Ramayana* (Bombay: Bharatiya Vidya Bhavan, 1952), pp. 219–21; condensed and cited with modifications.
4. Trans. from Tamil by A. K. Ramanujan, *Hymns for the Drowning: Poems for Visnu by Nammalvar* (Princeton, N.J.: Princeton University Press, 1981), p. 30.
5. From a pamphlet, "Sri Aurobindo Ashram, Delhi Branch" (Delhi: Matri Press, 1986), p. i.
6. M. N. Srinivas, *The Remembered Village* (New York: Oxford University Press, 1976), pp. 326–28; cited with modifications.
7. Trans. from Sanskrit by Jean Varenne in his *Yoga and the Hindu Tradition;* trans. from French by Derek Coltman (Chicago: University of Chicago Press, 1976), pp. 221–22.
8. David M. Miller and Dorothy C. Wertz, *Hindu Monastic Life: The Monks and Monasteries of Bhubaneswar* (Montreal-London: McGill-Queen's University Press, 1976), p. 103
9. Rabindranath Tagore, *A Flight of Swans: Poems from Balaka,* trans. from Bengali by Aurobindo Bose (London: John Murray, 1962), p. 107.
10. *Times of India,* New Delhi, December 11, 1987.

Glossary

Names and terms in the text have been simplified at the expense of accuracy in transliteration and pronunciation. For example, the *sh* in Vishnu and Shiva are not the same sounds and letters in spoken and written Sanskrit, and the vowels in Sita are long whereas in Indra they are short. In this Glossary and accompanying list of Deities, Powers, and Deified Heroes the standard diacritics have been added as a guide to pronunciation and for ease of recognition in further studies of Hinduism. All terms and names, with the exception of the South Indian deities Ayyappan, Mariamman, and Murukan, are Sanskrit, the language of religion and philosophy for classical and modern Hinduism.

Macrons over vowels lengthen them: *ā* as in "father," *ī* as in "teen," *ū* as in "boot." Vocalic *ṛ* is close to the *ri* of "ring." The sibilant *s* as in "sow" is distinct from both *ṣ* and *ś* as in "sure" or "shine." A *c* is always *ch* as in "church." All aspirated consonants contain crisp following *h* as in "goat-herd," "hog-head," "head-hunter," "up-hill," "knob-hill." Other diacritics distinguish among additional variations in sounds and letters, but they are minor and need not detain us here. Contemporary languages in South Asia frequently drop the final *"a"* of terms that derive from Sanskrit, as for example, *āśram, darśan, maṭh, yug.*

ācārya. A spiritual teacher or preceptor; learned scholar of religious traditions. *See also* guru.

advaita. Nonduality; the philosophical premise made prominent in Vedānta by Śaṅkara that only *brahman* is real.

ahiṃsā. Noninjury to any life form.

āśrama. One of the four stages of life; a tranquil place suitable for the third and fourth stages; a retreat or hermitage.

ātman. The Self, Soul, Spirit that is eternal, surviving successive mortal bodies until *mokṣa* provides release.

avatāra. A descent, manifestation, incarnation of a deity, Viṣṇu, for example.

avidyā. The wrong knowledge, worldly wisdom, that is ignorance.

bhakti. Devotion to a deity, the most popular path to salvation.

brahmacārin. Vedic student who lives according to *brahman* in the first of four stages of life (*āśramas*).

bráhman. The eternal essence of the sacred word; later, ultimate reality, the imperishable absolute without *guṇas*; the Upaniṣads identify *ātman* with *brahman*. The *brahmán* is a supervisory priest for Vedic rituals.

brāhmaṇa varṇa. Highest of the three twiceborn classes, the traditional priestly rank of society; Brahman and Brahmin are common spellings.

darśana. Sight of a deity, sacred site, holy person; such vision transforms the seer.

dharma. Spiritual duty in accord with cosmic law and order; perhaps the closest Sanskrit world for "religion," *dharma* replaces Vedic term *ṛta*.

dhyāna. Meditation; in classical *yoga,* the state of awareness prior to *samādhi*.

dīkṣā. Ritual consecration, initiation.

gāyatrī. The initiatory *mantra* of a twiceborn Hindu (*Ṛgveda* 3.62.10).

gopi. One of the cowherd girls in love with Kṛṣna; in devotional poetry, songs, paintings, and instrumental music she is the human soul longing for God.

gṛhya. The household, domicile.

guṇa. "Strand," quality, attribute; the three strands of nature according to certain philosophies are purity, brightness (*sattva*), passion (*rajas*), inertia (*tamas*); a distinction often made is one between the impersonal absolute (*brahman*) without qualities (*nirguṇa*) and a personal absolute or supreme being with qualities (*saguṇa*).

guru. A teacher, spiritual guide. *See also* ācārya.

homa. An offering to a deity, especially one into a sacred fire.

iṣṭadevatā. Chosen deity, a god or goddess with whom a devotee maintains a special relationship.

japa. The repetition of divine names, *mantras*, or prayers.

jāti. A "kind" of being; a caste or caste-group in the social hierarchy. *See also* varṇa.

jīva. An individual form of life, being.

jñāna. Knowledge, particularly spiritual knowledge aquired by insight, the grace of a deity, or other nondiscursive means.

karma. Action; in the Vedas, ritual work; later *karma* comes to mean not only all action but the personal consequences or destiny that accrue from action. *See also* saṃsāra.

kṣatriya varṇa. Second of the three twiceborn classes, traditionally the warrior nobility of society.

līlā. The divine play or sport of a deity, Kṛṣṇa, for example.

liṅga. The phallus, major symbol of Śiva's regenerative powers.

loka. World-space.

maṇḍala. A diagram of circles and squares representing the cosmos for ritual and meditation. *See also* yantra.

mantra. An essential sound or phrase from *śruti;* later, any oral formula of sacred power.

mārga. Path, way, discipline leading to salvation.

maṭha. A study hall, sectarian school, monastery, or all three, often part of the institutional structure of an important temple.

māyā. The creative magic powers of a deity, Varuṇa or Kṛṣṇa, for example; cosmic illusion.

mokṣa. Release, freedom, liberation of the *ātman* from its bondage to *saṃsāra.*

phala. Fruit, consequence, result of sacrifice; in post-Vedic Hinduism, the fruit of all action, not ritual action alone.

prakṛti. Nature, primal matter, the phenomenal world with its three *guṇas;* the feminine complement/opposite of masculine *puruṣa.*

prāṇa. Breath, both cosmic and human; *prāṇāyāma* is yogic control of breathing.

prasāda. Grace, favor of a deity or holy person; the consecrated ritual remnant, the coconut, for example, broken before a goddess as offering, then returned to the offerer as food transformed by her grace.

pūjā. Worship of a deity, person, or object representing the sacred.

purohita. Domestic priest.

puruṣa. "Male," spirit; consciousness, the complement/opposite of feminine *prakṛti*.

ṛta. Cosmic order. *See also* dharma.

sādhu. A world renouncer, a wandering mendicant on a spiritual quest.

samādhi. A state of release, transcendence; eighth and highest stage in the process of classical *yoga;* the burial site of a holy person.

saṃnyāsa. Renunciation, the fourth and highest stage of life.

saṃsāra. This-worldly realm of rebirths; transmigration. *See also* karma.

saṃskāra. Perfection, rite of passage, life-cycle ritual.

śānti. Peace, tranquility.

smṛti. Tradition, memory, the total human recall of spiritual values; distinct from and dependent on its basis, the eternal *śruti*.

śrāddha. Funeral rites and subsequent offerings to ancestors.

śramaṇa. "Striver," non-Vedic ascetic or renunciant.

śruti, śrauta. Both from the verb "to hear," *śruti* being "that which is heard," that is, the Vedas, and *śrauta* being those rituals that maintain human-cosmic *links* according to *śruti,* the ultimate authority. *See also* smṛti.

śūdra varṇa. Fourth of the social classes, not among the twice-born; in many regions of India *śūdras* and the still lower Scheduled Castes and tribes are the majority of the population.

tapas. "Heat," austerities, ascetic techniques that are spiritually creative.

tyāga. Abandonment, relinquishment; a Vedic ritual term that came to mean a letting go of the fruits of action.

upanayana. Initiation by investiture with a sacred thread and instruction in Vedic *mantras* and offerings.

vāhana. An animal, bird, or other mount of a deity.

vaiśya varṇa. Third of the three twiceborn classes, traditionally concerned with productivity (domestic animals, agriculture, certain crafts), but today calling to mind the merchants.

varṇa. One of the four classes of humans in the social hierarchy; each includes numerous *jātis*.

veda. Sacred knowledge, collection of revealed texts made known to the ancient seers.

vrata. Personal vow, often connected with fasting, pilgrimage, donations, particular *pūjās* or austerities.

yajña. Sacrifice, the ritual work (*karma*) of Vedic priests on behalf of the sacrificer and the world.

yantra. Mystical diagram of cosmic powers. *See also* maṇḍala.

yoga, yogi. Yoking of the self by spiritual discipline (*yoga*) creates of an ordinary human a spiritually disciplined one (*yogin*).

yuga. One of the four ages of cosmic timekeeping: Kṛta, Tretā, Dvāpara, and the (present) Kali *yuga*.

Deities, Powers, and Deified Heroes

Aditi. Vedic goddess, boundless mother of the gods, especially of the eight or twelve Ādityāṇs, including Mitra, Varuma, and Indra.

Agni. The Vedic sacrificial fire and god of fire.

apsaras. One of the host of beautiful celestial maidens; consorts of *gandharva*s.

Arjuna. Warrior hero of the *Mahābhārata* epic; celebrated for his dialogue with Kṛṣṇa in the *Bhagavad Gītā.*

asura. An early Vedic term for sovereign deity or "lord"; in subsequent mythology the *asura*s are collective demonic powers opposed to the *deva*s.

Aśvins. Twin "horsemen" in the Vedas, divine physicians, comparable in some respects to the Greek Dioskuroi.

Ayyappaṉ. A son of Śiva and a female incarnation of Viṣṇu; related mythically to Skanda and Kārttikeya; popular in South India, where his principal locus is the Sabari Hill (Sabarimala).

Balarāma. Older brother of Kṛṣṇa.

Brahmā. The creator, grandfather (that is, the oldest) of the gods; perpetuates in epics and *purāṇas* only a shadow of the supreme being Puruṣa-Prajāpati of the early Vedic texts.

bhūta. Ghost, particularly a troublesome or malevolent spirit of the dead, likely to possess people.

deva. "God"; generic name for Vedic and later deities.

Draupadī. Heroine-goddess of the *Mahābhārata* epic and wife of the five Pāṇḍava brothers.

devī. Feminine form of *deva* and generic name for "goddess"; regional names and forms are countless; in the epics and *purāṇas* Cāmuṇḍā, Durgā, Gaurī, Kālī, Lakṣmī, Mahādevī, Pārvatī, Sarasvatī, Śrī, and Umā are prominent, among others.

Durgā. A fierce, aggressive goddess, celebrated for her killing of Mahiṣāsura; worshiped in two great annual festivals.

gandharva. One of the host of male celestial musicians; consorts of *apsarasa*s.

Gaṇeśa. Also known as Gaṇapati, "lord of the hosts (of devotees)," or Vināyaka; the elephant-headed remover of obstacles, he is a son of Śiva and Pārvatī.

Garuḍa. The eagle or hawk mount of Viṣṇu; enemy of the *nāga*s.

Hanumat or **Hanuman.** Monkey hero and ally of Rāma in the *Rāmāyaṇa* epic; popular for his demonstrative devotion and loyalty, as well as courageous guardianship.

Indra. Heroic warrior god, most dynamic of Vedic deities, drinker of soma and slayer of Vṛtra; king of the gods in pre-epic mythology.

Kālī. Terrible goddess, black in color and bloodthirsty in action, provider and taker of all life forms; recipient of blood sacrifice—goats, for example.

Kṛṣṇa. The dark blue or black god, celebrated in mythic episodes as mischievous child, heroic slayer of demons, lover of the cowgirls (*gopi*s), king; an *avatāra* of Viṣṇu and principal figure in two of the most popular of texts, the *Bhāgavata purāṇa* and the *Bhagavad gītā.*

kuṇḍalinī. A specific type of *śakti* in Tantric Yoga, a feminine serpent power coiled at the base of the spine, but raised by yogic techniques through the seven levels (*cakra*s) of the human-cosmic body.

Lakṣmana. Younger brother of Rāma.

Lakṣmī. Goddess of good fortune, wealth, prosperity; wife of Viṣṇu.

lokapāla. Guardian of the universe; four, sometimes eight, are stationed at the directions, for example, Indra (east), Kubera (north), Varuṇa (west), Yama (south).

Mahiṣa or Mahiṣāsura. The buffalo god/demon slain by Durgā (Devī); possibly a pre-Vedic deity, he is still worshiped in South India, as Pōtu Rāja, the Buffalo King, for example.

Manu. Progenitor of humankind; the *purāṇa*s elaborate on each of the Manu-s to appear in the successive periods (*manvantara*s) of cosmic time.

Māriammaṉ. Prominent goddess of epidemic disease in South India.

Marut. One of the storm gods, militant troops of Rudra. *See also* Rudra.

Murukaṉ. Popular deity in Tamil Nadu, identified with Skanda-Kārttikeya.

nāga. Serpent god/demon; mythically related to autochthonous peoples of South Asia.

Nandin. The bull mount of Śiva; celebrated for his devotion and guardianship.

Narasiṃha. The "man-lion" *avatāra* of Viṣṇu, a fierce form of this otherwise benign deity.

navagraha. One of the nine planets: Sūrya (Sun), Candra (Moon), Maṅgala (Mars), Budha (Mercury), Guru or Bṛhaspati (Jupiter), Śukra (Venus), Śani (Saturn), and the mythical invisible planets of eclipses, Ketu and Rāhu; all are males; the last three are dark and dangerous; shrines, temples, calendars, horoscopes, talismans, and rings reflect their significance.

Pāṇḍava. One of the five sons of Paṇḍu, heroes of the *Mahābhārata* epic: Yudhiṣṭhira, Arjuna, Bhīma, and the twins Nakula and Sahadeva.

Pārvatī. Goddess-daughter of the mountain, chaste wife and passionate lover of Śiva.

piśāca. A flesh-eating demon, one of the hordes that haunt cremation and burial grounds.

pitṛ. "Father," that is, an ancestor, one of the community of the departed, male and female, who receive offerings of food, water, and *mantra*s.

Prahlāda. Famous devotee of Viṣṇu rescued from his murderous demon-father Hiraṇyakaśipu by the Narasiṃha *avatāra* of Viṣṇu.

Prajāpati. "Lord of creatures," the Vedic creator-god who perpetuates in the Brāhmaṇas the self-sacrificing creation of Puruṣa in the *Ṛgveda;* his ascetic fervor (*tapas*) is the origin of beings.

Pṛthivī. The female Earth; paired in early Vedic myths with Dyaus, the masculine Sky or Heaven.

Puruṣa. The primordial sacrifice-Person (*puruṣa,* literally, "male"); he projects his dismembered parts into cosmic phenomena and also the four human classes, derived respectively from his mouth, arms, thighs, feet; *Ṛgveda* 10:90 is a famous hymn known as the Puruṣa-sūkta. *See also* Prajāpati.

rākṣasa. A terrible demon opposed to gods and heroes.

Rāma. Hero of the epic *Rāmāyaṇa,* king of Ayodhyā, husband of Sītā; considered the model of masculine virtue and power; an *avatāra* of Viṣṇu.

Rāvaṇa. Captor of Sītā and enemy of Rāma in the *Rāmāyaṇa* epic; a demon in the Sanskrit texts, he is considered a powerful deity in parts of South India.

ṛṣi. A "seer" or sage; the seven great sages who first apprehended the Vedas include the well-known Bharadvāja, Bhṛgu, Dakṣa, Kaśyapa, and Vasiṣṭha.

Rudra. Vedic god of the wilderness; his late-Vedic epithet Śiva, "auspicious," becomes his best known name. The Rudra-s are the eight or eleven troops of Rudra, including the major epithets of the classical god Śiva. *See also* Marut.

śakti. Feminine cosmic energy. *See also* kuṇḍalinī.

Sarasvatī. Goddess of wisdom and patroness of musicians, poets, artists, scholars; wife of Brahmā.

Satī. Daughter of Dakṣa and wife of Śiva; she immolated herself in a self-created sacrificial fire to protest her father's insult to Śiva; her name is also wrongly applied to the practice of widow self-immolation on the husband's funeral pyre.

Śeṣa or Ananta. The cosmic serpent on which Viṣṇu lies asleep.

Sītā. Heroine-goddess of the *Rāmāyaṇa* epic, wife of Rāma; as Rama is the ideal male, so is Sītā the model of feminine chastity, loyalty, devotion.

Śiva. The epic and purāṇic deity Rudra-Śiva, also known as Bhava, Hara, Īśānā, Mahādeva, Maheśvara, Naṭarāja, Paśupati, Śambhu, Śaṅkara; two of his terrible forms are Bhairava in North India and Vīrabhadra in South India.

Skanda. Also known as Kārttikeya, Kumāra, Subrahmaṇya; a bachelor son of Śiva, portrayed in iconography with six heads; in Tamil Nadu he is identified with Murukaṉ, and throughout South India shares certain aspects with Ayyappaṉ.

Soma. Sacred Vedic plant of poetic visions and immortality; a divine king immolated and sacrificed in the most exalted of Vedic rituals; his pressed juice (*soma*), offered to the gods and drunk by the priests, was said to produce ecstasy.

Sūrya. The Vedic god of the sun; Savitṛ is another name for the sun.

Uṣas. Vedic goddess of the dawn.

Vāc. Vedic goddess of speech, the sacred word.

Varuṇa. Vedic sovereign, celestial deity; king of the gods before Indra; often invoked along with Mitra, god of contracts.

Vayu. Vedic god of wind and warfare.

Viṣṇu. Vedic god connected with the all-pervasive cosmic pole, creative order, and the energy of the sacrifice; in post-Vedic mythology he is known by many names, including Bhagavan, Hari, Nārāyaṇa, and Vasudeva; his manifestations (*avatāras*) include powerful independent deities such as Kṛṣṇa, Rāma, Narasiṃha, and the boar Varāha.

Vṛtra. The cosmic serpent who withholds creative waters; slain by Indra in a famous cosmogonic combat described in the *Ṛgveda*.

yakṣa, yakṣī. Respective male and female powers of fertility and abundance; Kubera, god of wealth and one of the *lokapālas*, is chief of the *yakṣas*.

Yama. First human, born before his twin sister Yamī; the first to die and therefore lord of the dead and, later, judge of the dead.

Selected Reading List

Literature in English Translation

Dimmitt, Cornelia, and J. A. B. van Buitenen (ed., tr.). *Classical Hindu Mythology: A Reader in the Sanskrit Puranas.* Philadelphia: Temple University, 1978.

Edgerton, Franklin (tr.). *The Beginnings of Indian Philosophy.* Cambridge, Mass.: Harvard University Press, 1965.

Miller, Barbara Stoler (tr.). *Love Song of the Dark Lord: Jayadeva's* Gitagovinda. New York: Columbia University Press, 1977.

O'Flaherty, Wendy Doniger (tr.). *The* Rig Veda: *An Anthology.* Baltimore, Md.: Penguin, 1981.

——— (tr.). *Hindu Myths: A Sourcebook Translated from the Sanskrit.* Baltimore, Md.: Penguin, 1975.

——— (ed. and tr.). *Textual Sources for the Study of Hinduism.* Manchester: Manchester University Press, 1988.

Ramanujan, A. K. (tr.). *Hymns for the Drowning: Poems for Visnu by Nammalvar.* Princeton, N.J.: Princeton University Press, 1981.

Sources of Indian Tradition. 2 vols. 2d ed. New York: Columbia University Press, 1988. Vol. 1, *From the Beginning to 1800*, ed. Ainslee T. Embree. Vol. 2, *Modern India and Pakistan*, ed. Stephen Hay.

Van Buitenen, J. A. B. (tr.). *The* Bhagavadgita *in the* Mahabharata: *A Bilingual Edition.* Chicago: University of Chicago Press, 1981.

General Surveys

Basham, A. L. *The Origins and Development of Classical Hinduism*. Ed. Kenneth R. Zysk. Boston: Beacon, 1989.

———. *The Wonder That Was India*. New York: Grove, 1954.

——— (ed.). *A Cultural History of India*. New York: Oxford Univeristy Press, 1984.

Brockington, J. L. *The Sacred Thread: Hinduism in its Continuity and Diversity*. Edinburgh: Edinburgh University Press, 1981.

Hopkins, Thomas J. *The Hindu Religious Tradition*. Encino. Calif.: Dickenson, 1971.

Kinsley, David. *Hinduism: A Cultural Perspective*. Englewood Cliffs, N.J.: Prentice Hall, 1982.

Sivaraman, Krishna (ed.). *Hindu Spirituality: Vedas through Vedanta*. New York: Crossroads, 1989.

Zaehner, R. C. *Hinduism*. New York: Oxford University Press, 1962.

Special Topics

Allchin, Bridget, and Raymond Allchin. *The Rise of Civilization in India and Pakistan*. New York: Cambridge University Press, 1982.

Alper, Harvey P. (ed.). *Mantra*. Albany: State University of New York, 1989.

Babb, Lawrence A. *The Divine Hierarchy: Popular Hinduism in Central India*. New York: Columbia University Press, 1975.

Blackburn, Stuart H., and A. K. Ramanujan (eds.). *Another Harmony: New Essays on the Folklore of India*. Berkeley and Los Angeles: University of California Press, 1986.

Carman, John. *The Thoelogy of Ramanuja*. New Haven: Yale University Press, 1974.

Courtright, Paul B. *Ganesa: Lord of Obstacles, Lord of Beginnings*. New York: Oxford University Press, 1985.

Daniel, E. Valentine. *Fluid Signs: Being a Person the Tamil Way.* Berkeley and Los Angeles: University of California Press, 1984.

Das, Veena. *Structure and Cognition: Aspects of Hindu Caste and Ritual.* New York: Oxford University Press, 1977.

Dasgupta, Surendranath. *A History of Indian Philosophy.* 5 vols. Cambridge: Cambridge University Press, 1922–55.

Deutsch, Eliot. *Advaita Vedanta: A Philosophical Reconstruction.* Honolulu: University of Hawaii Press, 1969.

Dumont, Louis. *Homo hierarchicus: The Caste System and Its Implications.* Trans. Mark Sainsbury, Chicago: University of Chicago Press, 1970.

Eck, Diana. *Darsan: Seeing the Divine Image in India.* 2d ed. Chambersburg, Pa.: Anima, 1985.

Eliade, Mircea. *Yoga: Immortality and Freedom.* Trans. Willard R. Trask, 2d ed. Princeton, N.J.: Princeton University Press, 1969.

Gonda, Jan. *Visnuism and Sivaism: A Comparison.* London: Athlone, 1970.

Gupta, Sanjukta; Dirk Jan Hoens; and Teun Goudrianan. *Hindu Tantrism.* Leiden: E. J. Brill, 1979.

Hardy, Friedhelm. *Viraha-Bhakti: The Early History of Krsna Devotion in South India.* New York: Oxford University Press, 1983.

Hawley, John S. *Krishna, the Butter Thief.* Princeton, N.J.: Princeton University Press, 1983.

Heesterman, J. C. *The Inner Conflict of Tradition: Essays in Indian Ritual, Kingship, and Society.* Chicago: University of Chicago Press, 1985.

Hiltebeitel, Alf. *The Ritual of Battle: Krishna in the* Mahabharata. Ithaca, N.Y.: Cornell University Press, 1976.

——— (ed.). *Criminal Gods and Demon Devotees: Essays on the Guardians of Popular Hinduism.* Albany: State University of New York, 1989.

Jayakar, Pupul. *The Earthen Drum: An Introduction to the Ritual Arts of Rural India.* New Delhi: National Museum, 1980.

Kane, P. V. *History of Dharmasastra.* 5 vols. 2d ed. Poona: Bhandarkar Oriental Research Institute, 1968–75.

Khare, Ravindra S. *The Hindu Hearth and Home*. Durham, N.C.: Carolina Academic, 1976.

Kinsley, David. *Hindu Goddesses: Visions of the Divine Feminine in the Hindu Religious Tradition*. Berkeley and Los Angeles: University of California Press, 1986.

Kramrisch, Stella. *The Hindu Temple*. 2 vols. Calcutta, 1946; rpt. New Delhi: Motilal Banarsidass, 1976.

Lincoln, Bruce. *Myth, Cosmos, and Society: Indo-European Themes of Creation and Destruction*. Cambridge, Mass.: Harvard University Press, 1986.

Lingat, Robert. *The Classical Law of India*. Trans. J. Duncan M. Derrett. Berkeley and Los Angeles: University of California Press, 1973.

Marriott, McKim (ed.). *India through Hindu Categories*. New Delhi and Newbury Park, Calif.: Sage Publications, 1990.

O'Flaherty, Wendy Doniger. *The Origins of Evil in Hindu Mythology*. Berkeley and Los Angeles: University of California Press, 1976.

——— (ed). *Karma and Rebirth in Classical Indian Traditions*. Berkeley and Los Angeles: University of California Press, 1980.

Pocock, D. F. *Mind, Body, and Wealth: A Study of Belief and Practice in an Indian Village*. Oxford: Basil Blackwell, 1973.

Schwartzberg, Joseph E. (ed.). *A Historical Atlas of South Asia*. Chicago: University of Chicago Press, 1978.

Shulman, David D. *Tamil Temple Myths: Sacrifice and Divine Marriage in the South Indian Saiva Tradition*. Princeton, N.J.: Princeton University Press, 1980.

Singer, Milton. *When a Great Tradition Modernizes*. New York: Praeger, 1972.

——— (ed.). *Krishna: Myths, Rites and Attitudes*. Chicago: University of Chicago Press, 1969.

Smith, Brian K. *Reflections on Resemblance, Ritual, and Religion*. New York: Oxford University Press, 1989.

Staal, Frits. *Agni: The Vedic Ritual of Fire*. 2 vols. Berkeley, Calif.: Asian Humanities Press, 1983. Vol. 2 ed. Staal.

Stevenson, Margaret Sinclair. *The Rites of the Twice-Born*. London: Oxford University Press, 1920.

Varenne, Jean. *Yoga and the Hindu Tradition*. Trans. Derek Coltman. Chicago: University of Chicago Press, 1976.

Waghorne, Joanne Punzo, and Norman Cutler (eds.). *Gods of Flesh Gods of Stone: The Embodiment of Divinity in India*. Chambersburg, Pa.: Anima, 1985.

Welbon, Guy R., and Glenn E. Yocum (eds.). *Religious Festivals in South India and Sri Lanka*. Delhi: Manohar, 1982.

Zelliot, Eleanor, and Maxine Berntsen (eds.). *The Experience of Hinduism: Essays on Religion in Maharashtra*. Albany: State University of New York, 1988.

Zimmer, Heinrich. *Myths and Symbols in Indian Art and Civilization*. Ed. Joseph Campbell. New York: Bollingen Foundation, 1946; rpt. Princeton, N.J.: Princeton University Press, 1972.

Zvelebil, Kamil V. *The Smile of Murugan: On Tamil Literature of South India*. Leiden: E. J. Brill, 1973.